Barcode in Back

Criminal Justice
Recent Scholarship

Edited by
Marilyn McShane and Frank P. Williams III

A Series from LFB Scholarly

Police Use of Excessive Force in Disorganized Neighborhoods

Zachary R. Hays

LFB Scholarly Publishing LLC
El Paso 2011

Library of Congress Cataloging-in-Publication Data

Hays, Zachary R., 1980-
  Police use of excessive force in disorganized neighborhoods / Zachary
R. Hays.
       p. cm. -- (Criminal justice : recent scholarship)
   Includes bibliographical references and index.
   ISBN 978-1-59332-449-0 (pbk. : alk. paper)
   1. Police brutality--United States. 2. Community policing--United
States. 3. Neighborhoods--United States. I. Title.
   HV8141.H39 2011
   363.2'3--dc22

                                              2010052921

ISBN 978-1-59332-449-0

Printed on acid-free 250-year-life paper.

Manufactured in the United States of America.

TABLE OF CONTENTS

LIST OF TABLES

vii

LIST OF FIGURES

ACKNOWLEDGEMENTS

My sincerest appreciation goes out to all my family and friends – none of this would have been possible without your love and support. Special thanks go out to my wonderful wife, Rachael, who has stood by me all these years. Finally, special thanks also to Eric Silver, D. Wayne Osgood, Barrett Lee, Eric Plutzer, and Stephen Mastrofski for all their years of advice and mentorship.

CHAPTER 1
Neighborhoods & Police Use of Force

The scholarly literature on police officers' use of force has expanded over the past few decades, yet there remains relatively little theory that explains such police behavior. The vast majority of policing studies remain atheoretical, and those studies that are theory-driven tend to rely on only two broad theoretical frameworks – *social threat theories* and *criminal threat theories*. While these frameworks have been established as strong explanations for police use of force, if the field is to move forward, alternative explanations must be put forth and empirically tested. This book fills this conspicuous gap in the literature by proposing the appropriation of the criminological theory of social disorganization (typically used to explain rates of crime) and then empirically testing it as possible explanation for police use of force behaviors.

Shaw and McKay's (1942) theory of social disorganization has traditionally been used to explain the high rates of crime commonly found in inner-city neighborhoods. Born out of the Chicago School's tradition of neighborhood ecology, Shaw and McKay viewed crime as the result of neighborhood contextual factors rather than the individual-specific factors that had previously garnered the attention of most criminologists. Although the relevance and popularity of Shaw and McKay's social disorganization theory has fluctuated over the years in the eyes of many criminologists, the role of neighborhood context has only very recently come to the attention of policing researchers. Two of the first researchers to consider how neighborhood context might influence police behavior were Slovak (1986) and Smith (1986), only forty years after Shaw and McKay's original research. Slovak perfectly captured both researchers' sentiment when he lamented that "there is no solid lead to follow from the research of others in this regard, for almost no serious efforts to tie ecological variations within a city to police patterns in particular or to social control efforts in general have yet appeared" (1986:144).

1

In one of only a handful of empirical studies that have examined neighborhood context and police use of force since Slovak's statement, Terrill and Reisig (2003) similarly commented that, "the literature dealing specifically with police use of force [in regards to neighborhood context] is even more remote" (294). Then, in an effort to rectify that gap in the literature, the two researchers conducted an empirical examination of neighborhood context and police use of force. Unfortunately, while Terrill and Reisig observed a significant relationship between the two phenomena, they failed to embrace a theoretical framework as the driving force behind their research.[1] Consequently, despite their step in the right direction, without using a theoretical framework to explain *how* and *why* neighborhood context might influence police behavior (and police use of force, in particular), we are no closer to truly understanding the relationship.

Despite the lack of theory in Terrill and Reisig's (2003) empirical research, though, there has been some effort by at least one policing researcher to theoretically explain how neighborhoods affect police actions. Six years prior to Terrill and Reisig's empirical study of neighborhood context and police use of force, Klinger (1997) noted that "few studies have considered the possibility that police action might vary across urban neighborhoods . . . [and] none contains any systematic theory linking police activity to the ecological contexts in which it occurs" (278). In an effort to address this issue, he therefore proposed an ecological theory of police behavior that focused on how ecological (i.e. neighborhood) context might affect the vigor with which police officers did their jobs.[2] In other words, Klinger proposed a theoretical explanation for how hard police officers worked, and how thoroughly they carried out their duties, based on variations in neighborhood characteristics. Unfortunately, however, he never applied his ecological theory to specifically explaining police use of force behaviors. Furthermore, he has never, to this date, attempted to empirically assess the validity of his theory. Consequently, even though policing researchers have independently begun to both empirically examine and theorize about the nature of the relationship between neighborhood context and police use of force, a *theory-driven empirical analysis* has yet to be conducted.

---

[1] This study is reviewed in more detail in Chapter 3.

[2] This study is reviewed in more detail in Chapter 2.

This book echoes the sentiments made by Slovak, Terrill, Reisig, and Klinger - it is essential that policing researchers explore the role of neighborhood context in regards to explaining how and why police officers' use force against the civilian residents of those neighborhoods. Unlike previous research, however, the research presented in this book combines a theoretical framework for understanding the influence of neighborhood context on police officers' use of force with a rigorous empirical test of that framework. For the purposes of this study, the *social disorganization tradition* that was founded by Shaw and McKay in the 1930s and 1940s serves as the foundation for a new social disorganization theory of police use of force.

Since Shaw and McKay's (1942) original theory of social disorganization, the *tradition* of their research has lived on through the works of many other neighborhoods and crime researchers, including an increased emphasis on the role of neighborhood informal social control efforts (Kornhauser 1978), the rise of the neighborhood systemic model (Bursik and Grasmick 1993; Hunter 1985; Sampson and Groves 1989), and most recently, the emergence of the neighborhood collective efficacy perspective (Morenoff, Sampson, and Raudenbush 2001; Sampson, Morenoff, and Earls 1999; Sampson, Raudenbush, and Earls 1997). It is this more broadly-defined *social disorganization tradition*, rather than just Shaw and McKay's social disorganization theory as they originally conceived of it, that is adapted to help explain police officers' use of force in different neighborhoods, with a special emphasis on Sampson and colleagues' concept of neighborhood collective efficacy (Morenoff et al. 2001; Sampson et al. 1999; Sampson et al. 1997).

To understand how and why neighborhood context might influence police officers' use of force, one must first understand the arguments made within the social disorganization tradition, however. Briefly, Shaw and McKay (1942) originally conceived of neighborhood social disorganization as the inability of neighborhood residents to collectively define and achieve common goals, such as the prevention of crime. They argued that neighborhood social disorganization resulted from deteriorating conditions within neighborhoods related to increasing rates of poverty, racial and ethnic heterogeneity (i.e., diversity), and residential instability (i.e., turnover). These factors, they posited, reduced the ability of neighborhood residents to informally control juveniles' delinquent behaviors and also helped to foster criminal values and gangs. In turn, Shaw and McKay believed that it was those characteristics that ultimately led to increased rates of juvenile delinquency in disorganized neighborhoods.

Decades later, Sampson and colleagues' (Morenoff et al. 2001; Sampson et al. 1999; Sampson et al. 1997) extension of Shaw and McKay's original social disorganization led to their collective efficacy approach, which is also of particular interest for this research. Sampson and colleagues' concept of collective efficacy differs from Shaw and McKay's original theory by combining residents' ability to informally control juveniles' delinquent behaviors with the level of social cohesion amongst neighbors. Subsequently, they defined collective efficacy as the mutual trust and solidarity among neighbors (social cohesion) necessary for individual residents to willingly intervene on behalf of the neighborhood whenever inappropriate or unacceptable behaviors arose (informal social control).

Based on the ideas and concepts described above, the object of this book is to establish (and test) a social-disorganization-tradition-based explanation of why police officers use force. This adapted theory argues that residents of disorganized neighborhoods, especially those with low levels of collective efficacy, will not only be vulnerable to higher rates of crime (as predicted by the social disorganization tradition), but they may also be vulnerable to higher rates of police use, and even abuse, of force. Specifically, it is expected that police officers working in disorganized neighborhoods will begin to use *excessive* levels of force as they come to realize that the residents of those neighborhoods are no more able to stop their inappropriate behavior than they are able to stop other undesirable behaviors (i.e., crime and delinquency).[3]

---

[3] It is not argued nor expected, that all, or even most, police officers will consciously choose to abuse their authority and use excessive levels of force in socially disorganized neighborhoods. Rather, it is expected that officers will begin to use more force than is ordinarily necessary in order to accomplish their duties as quickly and easily as possible in neighborhoods that also tend to be very dangerous. The link between neighborhood disorganization and police use of excessive force is discussed in more detail in Chapter 4.

Because this research focuses on explaining one type of police behavior particular, police use of excessive force, it is important to understand what exactly *excessive force* means. Following the lead of many other policing researchers, excessive force is defined as the use of any force that is beyond what is necessary to control an individual or effect the arrest of a suspect, including the use of any force when none is required (for a detailed discussion of how excessive force is defined, see Geller and Toch 1996). Based on this definition, an adapted social disorganization explanation of police use of force would then expect that the residents of socially disorganized neighborhoods are doubly-victimized, not only by the increased criminal activity in their neighborhoods, but also by some rogue police officers who use excessive force, and ultimately leaving them with nowhere to turn.

Research Objectives & Contributions

The main objectives of this research are to present a new theoretical explanation for police use of force behavior and to determine whether this explanation is empirically viable. In order to do so, the relationships between neighborhood context (e.g., structural conditions, social disorganization, the systemic model, and collective efficacy) and between-neighborhood variation in problems with police officers' use of excessive force are examined using data from Chicago, Illinois, during the 1990s. Then, based on the social disorganization tradition framework briefly discussed above, it is expected that highly disorganized neighborhoods not only experience higher rates of crime (as a large body of past research has already established),[4] but also higher rates of police use of excessive force.

In addition to adapting and empirically testing a new theoretical explanation for police use of force, a secondary objective of this research is to contribute to the theoretical and methodological

---

[4] For a review of this research, see Chapter 3. Since the relationship between neighborhood social disorganization and crime has already been well-established, that relationship is not examined empirically again. Instead, the focus of this research rests exclusively on the relationship between neighborhood social disorganization and police use of excessive force.

development of the literature on police use of force. Specifically, this research makes three important contributions to the field of policing. First, a detailed review of all of the theory-driven research on police use of force over the past 20 years is included in this book. The purpose of this review is to demonstrate the continued need for the development and testing of more theoretical research of police officers' use of force. Currently, the majority of research within the field is largely variable-driven, to the extent that many researchers have often simply included all the explanatory variables that they can find and then see what significant results come out the other end. Unfortunately, while such variable-driven studies can help us identify what factors are related to police officers' use of force, they cannot tell us anything about *why* those factors are related to police behavior. Consequently, such research does little to help us understand how such factors might be manipulated in order to help regulate police use of force.

Second, this research also contributes to the police use of force literature by improving upon the existing research methods that are commonly used within the field. Through the incorporation of a variety of neighborhood contextual measures, which are necessary to empirically test the adapted social disorganization tradition theory of police use of force, it becomes necessary to analyze police use of force at both the individual- and neighborhood-levels simultaneously. The majority of prior research on police use of force has been conducted exclusively at one level of analysis (i.e., either at the individual-level or the large-scale aggregate-level). Fortunately, however, recent advances in analytic methodologies now allow researchers to conduct analyses at multiple levels simultaneously. The research presented in this book takes advantage of such advanced methodologies and conducts a multi-level analysis of civilians' reports of police officers' use of excessive force that includes explanatory variables at both the individual- and neighborhood-levels. In doing so, this research introduces a new method through which policing researchers can utilize multi-level modeling techniques to account for potential measurement error issues associated with civilian reporting bias.

Finally, with few exceptions, researchers studying police officers' use of force have generally failed to incorporate neighborhood contextual factors into their studies. [5] Most examinations have tended

---

[5] See Chapter 4 for a review.

to focus either on individual-level predictors (e.g., officer and suspect characteristics) or on large-scale aggregate predictors (e.g., city-, state-, or even nationwide population characteristics). Very few studies have considered the importance of neighborhood context. By using a social disorganization tradition-based theoretical framework, this research provides a strong theoretical explanation of police use of force behaviors that recognizes the importance of neighborhoods. Through the incorporation of a variety of concepts traditionally used by researchers in the neighborhoods and crime literature, this book should not only open up many new avenues for theory-driven research that utilizes a whole new set of explanatory measures, it may also help us better understand the causes of police officers' use of force at the neighborhood level.

Given the above considerations, this research fills several significant gaps in the police use of force literature, and may potentially serve as a catalyst for more theory-driven, methodologically advanced, studies of neighborhoods and any variety of police behaviors. Then, as researchers gain a more thorough understanding of the factors that influence police behavior, that understanding can be passed along to police officials and administrators, who can in turn better educate the officers who work out in the field. In the end, the primary objective of this research is not only to get academics and policing researchers to consider new possibilities for their own studies, but also to help both police officers and civilians better understand how neighborhood contextual factors can affect the ways in which both groups interact with each other, especially in situations where the use of force may result.

CHAPTER 2
Current Explanations of Police Use of Force

Before discussing how the social disorganization tradition can be adapted to explain police use of force, it is necessary to understand how policing researchers currently attempt to explain such behavior. As briefly mentioned in Chapter 1, policing researchers have long lamented not only the paucity of theoretical explanations for police behaviors, but also the empirical research that might utilize such explanations as the driving force behind their work (e.g., Bernard and Engel 2001; Garner, Maxwell, and Heraux 2002; Hagan 1989; Klinger 2004). This chapter therefore reviews all of the major *theory-driven* studies of police use of force in the last twenty years[6], in order to help illustrate the continued need for theory (conceptualization and testing) in the policing literature.

One might ask, however, of what consequence is the use of a theoretical framework in policing research? That is, what is the big deal about conducting theory-driven research? Perhaps not surprisingly, many policing researchers agree with such a sentiment. In fact, many, if not most, empirical studies of police behavior are driven primarily by the availability of data and by examining interesting combinations of explanatory and outcome variables. And, while such

---

[6] The review contained here is restricted to research conducted over the past twenty years in order to limit this chapter to a reasonable length. Additionally, briefly reviewed throughout this chapter, the historical evidence (prior to twenty years ago) has largely produced results similar to the results found in the studies that are reviewed here. Finally, because the research that has been conducted in the last twenty years has the additional benefit of using more sophisticated methodologies and analytic techniques, such research can generally provide more reliable and accurate estimates of how various explanatory variables influence police officers' use of force. This review of the theory-driven empirical tests of existing police use of force theories is therefore limited to the research conducted since the late 1980s.

research can inform us about *which* factors may be related to police officers' use of force, they cannot explain *why* those factors are related to police officers' use of force. Absent such explanations, studies of this nature cannot help us understand how those factors might be manipulated to help control or reduce police officers' use of force.

For example, if researchers know that neighborhood rates of violence are positively related to police use of force, they might propose that we reduce poverty so that we may also reduce incidents of police use of force. Reducing violence is not so simple a matter, however. If it were, we would have done so a long time ago, for a host of different reasons. Subsequently, simply knowing that violence and police use of force are related can do little to influence "real world" policy without theory to explain why the phenomena are related.

If, on the other hand, some Theory X tells us that increased rates of violence leads to increased levels of strain amongst police officers, and then that increased strain leads to a higher likelihood of police use of force, then researchers can propose new policies for helping officers deal with the stress of their jobs. Thus, if policing researchers wish to truly have an influence on "real world" policy that might reduce unnecessary police use of force, it is necessary that they understand exactly why phenomena are related, not simply that they are. And, since one of the primary goals of this book is to further the theoretical development of the field, it is only those studies that have utilized a theoretical framework to test hypotheses regarding police officers' use of force (i.e., studies that are driven by theory) that are reviewed here.

Another important point to note before jumping into the review of theory-driven literature of the past 20 years is that even though the primary object of this book is to explain police officers' use of *excessive force*, it is useful to expand our focus here to include all types of police use of force behaviors, for two reasons. First, in comparison to the field in general, the number of studies focusing exclusively on police officers' use of *excessive* force is very limited. Second, whether it be the abuse of force (i.e., the use of excessive force), or the legitimate use of either lethal or non-lethal force, research on other forms of police use of force can still provide insight on why police officers' might use excessive force. In other words, if some precipitating factor is sufficient to provoke the legitimate use of (any kind of) force by the police, it may also be sufficient to provoke the use of excessive force by some police officers. Consequently, in an effort to better understand the reasons behind police use of force in general, this review includes studies of any, and all, forms of police use of force.

Theoretical Frameworks Explaining Police Use of Force

Nearly all of the theory-driven research on police use of force can be categorized into one of only two broad theoretical frameworks – *social threat theories* and *criminal threat theories*.[7] Studies that are driven by social threat theories generally argue that certain, less powerful, groups within the larger population pose a *social threat* to the existing power hierarchy, and therefore become the primary targets of formal social control efforts, including, but not limited to, police officers' use of force. Studies that are driven by criminal threat theories, on the other hand, generally argue that criminals, as well as other individuals, who pose a *criminal threat* to the physical safety of police officers or other civilians, become the primary targets of police officers' use of force so that their threats might be neutralized.

In addition to these two more popular theoretical frameworks, Klinger (1997) has recently proposed an ecological theory of police *vigor* which might be extended to explain police officers' use of force (although no one has attempted to do so thus far). Unfortunately, no empirical tests of Klinger's theory, as it relates to the explanation of

---

[7] Some might consider police organizational explanations of police officers' use of force to be a third theoretical framework for the study of police use of force. Unfortunately, no unified theoretical framework exists that connects the literatures on the various organizational factors that have been found to influence police use of force. That is, unlike studies testing other theoretical frameworks, there is no common theoretical argument that links organizational measures to police officers' use of force. Instead, researchers have only been able to identify a wide variety of measures (e.g. police subcultures, administrative or departmental use-of-force policies, officer training or experience, etc.) that all explain police use of force in different ways. Thus, generally speaking, any explanations based on various police organizational factors cannot and should not be considered true *theoretical frameworks* of police use of force.

either police vigor or police use of force, have been conducted to date. Nonetheless, as a possible avenue for the further theoretical development of police use of force literature, the basic tenets and arguments of his theory are reviewed in order to assess how they might be used to not only explain police vigor, but police use of force as well.

Social Threat Theories

Social threat theories were the first theories to be used by researchers to explain police officers' use of force, and can be traced back to Blalock's original theory of minority group relations (1967). Social threat theories generally include any explanations that focus on the formal social control (i.e., police use of force) of less powerful groups within a larger population. Among the more specific aggregate-level theories that fall under the broader heading of social threat theories are the conventional version of conflict theory (e.g., Jacobs 1979; Jacobs and Britt 1979; Sorensen, Marquart, and Brock 1993), the political threat hypothesis (e.g., Jacobs and O'Brien 1998), and racial or minority threat hypotheses (e.g., Blalock 1967; Blumer 1958; Bobo and Hutchings 1996; Holmes 2000). At the individual-level, social threat theories include Black's theory of law (Black 1976; Worden 1996), social script theory (Dwyer, Graesser, Hopkinson, and Lupfer 1990), and racial response bias arguments (e.g., Correll, Park, Judd, and Wittenbrink 2002; Correll, Park, Judd, Wittenbrink, Sadler, and Keesee 2007; Correll, Urland, and Ito 2006, Greenwald, Oakes, and Hoffman 2003).

Despite the variety of specific names of different social threat theories, they all generally contend that there is a conflict of interests among the different groups that make up any society, and that it is this conflict that leads to police use of force. More explicitly, social threat theories contend that in many stratified societies, but especially within western, capitalist societies such as our own, the powerful upper classes hold the financial, political, and, to a certain extent, moral authority which they can wield to protect their own interests. Unfortunately, however, the protection of the more powerful groups' interests usually comes at the expense of the interests of the less powerful groups. In regards to the police use of force, Jacobs (1979) argued that "the more there are inequalities in the distribution of economic power and economic resources, the more one can expect that the social control apparatus of the state will conform to the preferences of monied elites" (914). In another piece he continued, "[because] the state's monopoly of violence is controlled by those who benefit from inequality, it follows that the control agents of the state [i.e., the police] should be more likely to use extreme force when economic inequality is most pronounced" (Jacobs and Britt 1979:403). Thus, according to social threat theories, as tools or agents of the upper-class' interests, the police are expected to formally "control" members of the less powerful racial/ethnic and social class minority groups who pose a threat to the existing status hierarchy through all means available to them, including the use of physical force. Social threat theories therefore predict that members of minority groups will be more likely to experience police use of all kinds of force (legitimate and illegitimate, lethal and non-lethal) than members of majority groups.

Empirical Tests of Social Threat Theories

The empirical research testing social threat theories has typically utilized what policing researchers refer to as *extra-legal* variables to test their arguments. These variables measure various demographic characteristics of individuals that should have no legal bearing on how or why police officers use force (hence the *extra*-legal term). For example, researchers testing social threat theories commonly examine the effect of both aggregate- and individual-level measures of race/ethnicity, gender, age, or social class on police officers' use of force. Those researchers then argue that because it is against the interests of those who would benefit from society's inequalities (i.e., the majority groups who tend to hold power) for racial/ethnic minorities and lower-class individuals in particular to rise in power and/or numbers, those same individuals should be the most likely to experience police use of force. As such, the majority of the aggregate-level tests of social threat theories focus primarily on explaining variation in rates of police use of force via the size of racial/ethnic and social class minority populations, while individual-level tests focus on explaining how police officers differentially use force in encounters with racial/ethnic or social class minorities (to a lesser extent[8]) as compared to their encounters with whites and members of the social class majority.

Historically (prior to the set timeframe for this review), the empirical research testing both the aggregate- and individual-level effects of race/ethnicity and social class on police use of force has been supportive of the social threat theoretical framework (e.g., Binder and Fridell 1984; Binder and Scharf 1982; Blumberg 1986; Chamlin 1989; Goldkamp 1976; Hayden 1981; Horvath 1987; Jacobs and Britt 1979; Meyer 1980; Smith 1986). Like their historical counterparts, however, the large majority of the more recent empirical research testing social threat theories have also found that aggregate-level measures of race/ethnicity and social class, to a certain extent, are positively related to the police use of force. At the individual-level, the empirical research generally shows a similar pattern – that racial/ethnic minorities are more likely than whites to experience police officers' use of force (the effects of individual-level social class are less clear).

Aggregate-Level Evidence

In one of the most prominent tests of a social threat theory, Jacobs and O'Brien (1998) examined how black population size, income inequality, and racial inequality (white v. black median family income) were related to police use of deadly force across a large number of U.S. cities. The researchers extended Jacobs' earlier research, which also tested social threat theories (Jacobs 1979; Jacobs and Britt 1979), by examining justifiable police killings of civilians (i.e., police use of deadly force). Jacobs and O'Brien's dependent variable came from the FBI's Supplemental Homicide Report (SHR) for 170 cities nationwide with populations 100,000 or greater during the year of 1980. Data for their social threat explanatory measures came from the 1970 and 1980 U.S. census reports. Then, based on what they referred to as "political

---

[8] At the individual-level, very few studies test how suspects' social class influences police officers' use of force. This is due primarily to the fact that it is extremely difficult to operationalize and measure social class based solely on a suspect's appearance. Thus, most individual-level tests of social threat theories focus primarily on the effect of suspects' racial/ethnic background.

threat theory," Jacobs and O'Brien hypothesized that rates of police use of deadly force would be the greatest in cities where the black populations were the largest and where both income inequality in general and income inequality (i.e., social class inequality) between whites and blacks were the most pronounced.

In order to test their hypotheses, Jacobs and O'Brien conducted Tobit regression analyses to account for the heavily skewed distribution of their dependent variable. Because incidents of police use of deadly force were, and continue to be, extremely rare, many cities nationwide report zero incidents in any given year. Through the use of Tobit regression, the researchers were able to account for the skewed distribution of their police use of deadly force variable, and were able to obtain more accurate and unbiased estimates as a result. Additionally, the researchers conducted two separate Tobit regression analyses – one to test how city-level black population size, general income inequality, and racial income inequality were related to overall rates of police use of deadly force, and another to test how those same explanatory variables were related specifically to the rates of police killings of blacks.

Jacobs and O'Brien's first set of results revealed that only racial inequality was significantly and positively related to rates of police use of deadly force. Neither city-level black population size nor general income inequality were found to significantly predict changes in the overall rates of police use of deadly force. Interestingly, the results of their second set of analyses revealed that black population size was significantly and positively related to increased rates of police killings of blacks specifically. Thus, Jacobs and O'Brien's study provides only partial support for social threat theories. Unfortunately, however, because they did not examine how their explanatory variables might have been related to other, non-lethal, forms of police force, it is difficult to generalize their findings. That is, because police officers' use of deadly force is restricted specifically to situations in which a dangerous felon is attempting to escape (*Tennessee v. Garner,* 471 U.S. 1, 1985) variation in Jacobs and O'Brien's explanatory variables may have a very different affect other non-lethal, and less restricted, forms of police use of force, including police use of excessive force. Nonetheless, Jacobs and O'Brien's study is among one of the most methodologically sophisticated pieces of research examining police use of force to date, and is consequently one of the most often cited sources documenting (at least partial) support for social threat theories.

In another examination of rates of police use of deadly force, Sorensen and colleagues (1993) found much stronger support for the specific social threat theory that they tested. Like Jacobs and O'Brien, Sorensen and colleagues utilized data from the FBI's SHR on 170 cities with populations over 100,000, but instead examined rates of police use of deadly force over a period of five years (between 1980 and 1984). They also used 1980 U.S. census data to create their measures of social threat, which included city-level measures of overall income inequality (they used the GINI index where 0 indicates no inequality and 1 indicates complete inequality), black population size, and number of individuals living in poverty. Rather than testing political threat hypotheses, though, Sorensen and colleagues used the more traditional version of criminological conflict theory as the basis for three primary hypotheses: that cities with higher levels/larger populations of 1) income inequality, 2) black residents, and 3) impoverished residents would all experience higher rates of police use of deadly force as well.

Sorensen and colleagues used basic ordinary least squares (OLS) regression analyses to test their hypotheses. Unlike Jacobs and O'Brien (1998), however, Sorensen and colleagues did not adjust for the skewed distribution of their dependent variable. Instead, the researchers conducted a second set of analyses using only cities with populations over 250,000 which effectively circumvented their heteroskedasicity problem by removing a large number of the cities in their analysis that had reported zero incidents of police officers' use of deadly force. Despite their effort to account for such outlying cities, the researchers nonetheless observed similar results in both sets of analyses. They found that regardless of city size, all three of their measures of social threat were significantly and positively related to police killings of civilians. Consequently, unlike Jacobs and O'Brien's later study, Sorensen and colleagues' study provided strong support for social threat theories.

The fact that Sorensen and colleagues did not observe findings similar to those obtained later by Jacobs and O'Brien (1998) is somewhat surprising, especially given that both sets of researchers used largely the same data. One possible explanation for the differences in observed results between the two studies was Jacobs and O'Brien's use of Tobit regression techniques to correct for the skewed distribution of rates of police use of deadly force. However, Sorensen and colleagues conducted separate sets of analyses, in which they had essentially eliminated their heteroskedasicity problems (if only using a different method), and they still obtained significant results. The most likely explanation for the differences between the two studies is therefore the different measures of social threat that were used in each study, as well as the different control variables that were included in each study. That is, it is possible that Sorensen and colleagues found stronger support for social threat theories because they did not include any measures of racial income inequality, as did Jacobs and O'Brien. Regardless of differences between studies, however, both provide at least some support for a social threat theoretical framework of police use of force.

In the final theory-driven examination of rates of police use of deadly force conducted during the past 20 years, Liska and Yu (1992) found support for a social threat explanation as well. Unlike the two above studies, however, they used Vital Statistics data from the National Center for Health Statistics between 1975 and 1979 to construct their dependent variable. In a preemptive effort to avoid heteroskedasicity problems in their dependent variable, Liska and Yu included in their research only cities with populations of 250,000 or more, resulting in a total sample size of 45 cities. In addition to the Vital Statistics data, the researchers also constructed three social threat measures – city-level percent non-white, income inequality (the GINI index), and racial segregation (using a dissimilarity index to measure the percentage of whites who would have to move to another area to produce an even white to non-white population distribution). Based on what the researchers simply called "threat hypotheses," Liska and Yu hypothesized that all three of their social threat measures would be positively related to rates of police use of deadly force.

Liska and Yu tested their hypotheses using two sets of structural measurement models – one using their full sample, and one disaggregated by the race of the victim. The researchers found that percent non-white and racial segregation were two of the strongest predictors in both sets of analyses, net of a variety of controls, thereby providing support for social threat theories once again. Like Jacobs and O'Brien (1998), however, they found no effect of overall income inequality, in either set of analyses. As a result of the three studies reviewed thus far, it therefore appears that aggregate-level measures of race/ethnicity are better predictors of rates of police use of deadly force than are measures of income inequality.

In addition to the findings discussed above, Liska and Yu also found that percent non-white and racial segregation predicted similar rates of police use of deadly force for both whites and non-whites (there was once again no significant effect of income inequality). This finding stands in stark contrast to the findings of Jacobs and O'Brien (1998) that were described earlier. One possible explanation for the differences between these two studies is the different data and measures utilized by each set of researchers. Whereas Jacobs and O'Brien utilized SHR data to analyze rates of police use of deadly force on whites versus blacks in 1980, Liska and Yu utilized Vital Statistics data to analyze rates of police use of deadly force on whites versus non-whites during the 1970s. Consequently, it appears that while blacks were more likely to be victims of police officers' use of deadly force in 1980, racial/ethnic minorities as a whole (i.e. non-whites) were no more likely than whites to be the victim of police officers' use of deadly force during the 1970s. Regardless of these differences, however, Liska and Yu's research provides more (partial) support for social threat theories.

Moving away from the empirical tests of social threat theories that have focused on rates of police use of *deadly* force, Holmes (2000) examined how well social threat theories explained rates of police officers' use of *excessive* force. Data for his dependent variable came from the Department of Justice's (DOJ) Police Brutality Study (PBS), and measured the number of civilian complaints of police officers' use of excessive force that were reported to the DOJ between 1985 and 1990 (Holmes used the terms "police use of excessive force" and "police brutality" interchangeably). All cities with populations of 150,000 or larger that also had municipal police departments with at least two complaints of police use of excessive force annually were included in the study, for a total of 115 cities nationwide. Holmes' dependent variable was therefore the rate of civilian complaints of police use of excessive force per 100,000 individuals in the cities served by each municipal police department. In addition to the data from the PBS study, he also used census measures of city-level percent black, percent Hispanic, and racial income inequality (ratio of white to black and Hispanic median household incomes) to measure social threat.

Using the minority threat theory to guide him, Holmes then hypothesized that cities with larger black and Hispanic populations, and cities with higher levels of racial income inequality would have the highest rates of civilian complaints of police use of excessive force. Holmes tested his hypotheses using basic OLS regression analyses, and corrected for the non-normal distribution of his dependent variable through the use of Poisson estimation techniques. The results of his analyses revealed that that all three of his social threat measures were positively and significantly related to civilian complaints of police use of excessive force. Consequently, Holmes' study is the first to provide full support for social threat theories as explanations for non-lethal police use of force behaviors.

Unfortunately, though, Holmes was not able to distinguish between complaints made by members of minority groups and was therefore unable to determine whether or not the use of force by police was directed primarily at some groups in comparison to others (racial/ethnic and social class minorities vs. whites and social class majority members). Moreover, because his dependent variable relied on civilian reports of police use of force, he may have had measurement error problems in his dependent variable (resulting from civilian reporting bias) which could have affected his results.[9] Since Holmes did not account for the possibility of such problems, his results may subsequently be inaccurate. Nevertheless, because his results were generally consistent with the other tests of social threat theories that have already been reviewed here, it is unlikely that civilian reporting bias significantly affected Holmes' findings.

In another study examining police officers' use of excessive force, Smith and Holmes (2003) attempted to replicate Holmes' (2000) earlier findings using more sophisticated analytic techniques and an additional set of control variables. Like, Holmes' previous study, Smith and

---

[9] Civilian reports of police officers' use of excessive force are also utilized as measures of the dependent variable tested in this research, however, any potential measurement error in the dependent variable that might result from civilian reporting bias is held constant. For more details on how civilian reporting bias can be accounted for, see Chapter 5.

Holmes used the PBS and census data to create their dependent variable (rate of civilian complaints of police use of excessive force) and the same three social threat measures (city-level percent black, percent Hispanic, and racial income inequality). They also used the minority threat theory to propose the same hypotheses that Holmes tested earlier. In this study, however, Smith and Holmes included a number of organizational control variables to help determine whether or not the manner in which police departments handled civilian complaints of police use of excessive force might have influenced the rates at which they received those complaints. Additionally, instead of conducting Poisson-based OLS regression analyses, this time the researchers conducted negative binomial regression analyses to correct for the over-dispersion of their dependent variable.

Despite the changes from Holmes' (2000) earlier study, Smith and Holmes more refined analysis yielded generally similar results. That is, like Holmes (2000), the researchers found that both the city-level measures of percent black and percent Hispanic were positively and significantly related to rates of civilian complaints of police use of excessive force, net of a variety of controls, including the organizational measures related to how police departments handled civilian complaints. Unlike Holmes' earlier findings, however, in their more controlled model, the researchers were unable to replicate a significant effect of racial income inequality on civilian complaints. According to the researchers, this difference between study results was most likely due to their more conservative (i.e., more controlled) approach in the later study. Despite this distinction, Smith and Holmes were once again able to provide at least partial support for social threat theories of police use of force. Questions remain, however, regarding the role of racial income inequality. Even so, Smith and Holmes' study improved on Holmes' (2000) earlier study by conducting a more conservative test and provides more aggregate-level evidence that social threat theories can not only explain police officers' use of deadly force, but other forms of police use of force as well.

Individual-Level Evidence

Although many of the more well-known social threat theories (e.g., conflict, racial/minority threat, and political threat theories) are aggregate-level explanations of police use of force, a number of studies have sought to test the framework using individual-level data. These studies typically argue that police officers' (and society in general) tend to take a more punitive view toward, and generally have more negative conscious or unconscious biases against, racial/ethnic minorities, just as social threat theories would expect.[10] Overall, the individual-level tests of the social threat theoretical framework have been just as supportive as the aggregate-level studies, especially when it comes to the effect of race/ethnicity.

Much of the individual-level support for social threat theories come from simulation studies in which researchers used computers to assess how civilians (i.e., individuals who had no affiliation with the police or any police training) reacted differently in their decisions to use force against whites in comparison to racial/ethnic minorities. Unfortunately, since most of this research has not directly assessed the use of force responses of actual police officers, the findings of these studies should be considered only suggestive in nature. Nevertheless, the individual-level social threat theories that are at the core of these simulation studies argue that many police officers (just like all individuals within our society) may be prone to what some researchers have called "racial response bias" (Correll et al. 2002). According to these researchers, the concept of "racial response bias" explains how cultural stereotypes related to the negative perception of racial/ethnic minorities can manifest as involuntary or unconscious reactions that, given recognition, time, and training, may be effectively mediated. In the case of having to make split-second decisions in response to potentially dangerous situations, however, researchers expect that racial response bias may cause both police officers and civilians alike to be more likely to use force against minorities than against whites.[11] Thus,

---

[10] As previously mentioned, because it is difficult to operationalize and measure social class based solely at the individual-level, most of the individual-level empirical tests of social threat theories focus primarily on the effect of suspects' racial/ethnic background.

[11] Some might argue that some of the negative stereotypes about racial/ethnic minorities that persist in our culture may cause individuals to view them as being more dangerous. While such an argument might sound like it belongs in the *criminal* threat theories section discussed later in this chapter, racial

even though some of the studies reviewed below do not examine actual police officers' use of force behaviors, they can shed light on how police officers *might* respond.

Much of the simulation research on race/ethnicity and the use of force has been conducted by Correll and colleagues (Correll et al. 2002; Correll et al. 2007; Correll et al. 2006). In their two earlier studies (Correll et al. 2002; Correll et al. 2006), Correll and colleagues drew samples of undergraduate students from the University of Colorado and paid them eight dollars or gave them partial course credit to participate in their study (approximately 40 students for each study). After gathering their respective samples, the researchers then had the students play simple computer video games that presented the students with images of armed or unarmed, white or black, individuals. In the games, the researchers instructed the students to act as if they were police officers and that they should push a "shoot" button if they thought that the individual in the game was armed with a gun. Alternatively, the students were instructed to push a "don't shoot" button if they thought that the individual was holding some other non-weapon item (e.g., a bottle, cell phone, or wallet).

Based on the racial response bias argument discussed above, Correll and colleagues then hypothesized that the students in each study would be more likely to incorrectly choose to "shoot" at images of black individuals holding non-weapon items than images of white individuals holding non-weapon items, and that they would be more likely to correctly choose to "shoot" images of black individuals with guns than images of white individuals with guns.[12]

response bias arguments are inherently social threat theories. Social threat theorists would argue that the powerful groups in our society have the ability to influence how the racial/ethnic minority groups that pose a threat to the status quo should be viewed by the public (i.e., they can help perpetuate, if not actually create, the negative stereotypes surrounding racial/ethnic minorities). Subsequently, if conscious or unconscious racial response bias does affect individuals' decisions to use force, such evidence would be supportive of social threat theoretical framework, rather than criminal threat one.

[12] Correll and colleagues' "racial response bias" hypotheses are consistent with social threat theories, in that the researchers expect that many individuals within our society (obviously including, but not limited to just to police officers

In both studies, Correll and colleagues (Correll et al. 2002; Correll et al. 2006) found support for their racial response bias hypotheses. Using simple analysis of variance (ANOVA) techniques in each study, they observed that, on average, students were more likely to make the correct decision to "shoot" armed blacks, but were also more likely to incorrectly decide to "shoot" unarmed blacks. While the results of these studies are compelling, because the researchers used a non-random sample of compensated civilians, it is difficult to generalize their results to how true, trained, police officers might behave in real world situations. Additionally, the researchers only looked at the mean differences between outcomes (i.e., armed vs. unarmed and black vs. white), instead of conducting multivariate analyses in which they could have accounted for the effects of a variety of control variables (e.g., student participants' demographic characteristics). Subsequently, while the findings of these two earlier studies by Correll and colleagues are supportive of social threat theories in a more general sense, they nonetheless have a number of significant limitations that make their findings less compelling.

Around the same time that Correll and colleagues began their simulation tests, Greenwald and colleagues (2003) began a very similar study in a different part of the country. Greenwald and colleagues recruited 160 University of Washington undergraduate students to take part in a "virtual-reality weapons task" computer game. Unfortunately, the researchers provided no other information on how they obtained their sample (i.e., what sampling strategy they used, whether participants received any compensation, etc.). They do describe their virtual-reality game in detail, however. Similar to how Correll and colleagues implemented their studies (Correll et al. 2002; Correll et al. 2006), students in Greenwald and colleagues' study were also instructed to act as if they were undercover police officers. The researchers then directed the student participants to push a "shoot"

---

and university students) have unconscious biases toward racial/ethnic minorities which make them more prone to perceive them negatively. As a result of this racial response bias, Correll and colleagues expected that racial/ethnic minorities should be more likely to experience all types of formal social control, including police officers' use of deadly force.

button as quickly as possible if the individual displayed in the game was dangerous (i.e., holding a gun). Unlike the Correll and colleagues' studies, however, students also had the option to push a "safety" button if the individual shown in the game was a fellow officer. Finally, the students were also instructed that they could to do nothing if the individual shown in the game was actually just a non-dangerous civilian (i.e., not holding a gun).

Using the same racial response bias argument made by Correll and colleagues (Correll et al. 2002; Correll et al. 2006), Greenwald and his colleagues then hypothesized that their sample of students would similarly be more likely to incorrectly choose to "shoot" unarmed black individuals than they would be to correctly shoot armed white individuals. Unfortunately, Greenwald and colleagues did not explicitly discuss their analytic strategy. Despite this, based on what appeared to be simple comparisons of the proportions of whites incorrectly shot vs. blacks incorrectly shot, the researchers concluded that that both white and black students were more likely to incorrectly choose to shoot unarmed black individuals in their game. If we are to accept Greenwald and colleagues' somewhat questionable methods and findings then, their study was largely successful in replicating the results obtained by the two earlier Correll and colleagues pieces. But, like those studies, Greenwald and colleagues' research suffers from a number of limitations as well, including their use of university students instead of actual police officers and their lack of discussion regarding how they obtained their sample and what analytic strategy they utilized. As a result, it is difficult to draw hard conclusions about what affect race has on actual, trained police officers' decisions to "use force" in real world situations.

Fortunately, the most recent simulation study by Correll and colleagues (Correll et al. 2007) addressed many of the limitations of not only Greenwald and colleagues' study (2003), but of their own earlier studies as well (Correll et al. 2002; Correll et al. 2006). For this piece, the researchers recruited both civilians *and* two separate groups of sworn police officers to participate in their computer simulation experiments. They randomly recruited 135 civilians to voluntarily participate in the study with the help of Colorado Department of Motor Vehicle (each participant was paid $20). Then, in addition to their civilian sample, Correll and colleagues also recruited 124 officers from the Denver Police Department and 113 officers from across the country who were in Denver for a training seminar to voluntarily participate (each officer was paid $50). All 372 civilian and police officer participants were then instructed on how to play the same computer game simulation that Correll and colleagues used in their previous studies (Correll et al. 2002; Correll et al. 2006).

Once again, based on the racial response bias argument, Correll and colleagues (2007) hypothesized that all participants (i.e., both civilians and the two groups of police officers) would be more likely to incorrectly choose to "shoot" images of non-threatening blacks than non-threatening whites. For this study, however, they also hypothesized that the two groups of police officers would be less likely to make mistakes for both images of threatening and non-threatening whites *and* blacks (i.e., incorrectly choose to "shoot" images of unarmed individuals or incorrectly choose "not to shoot" images of armed individuals).

After all their participants had completed the simulation, Correll and colleagues once again conducted simple ANOVA tests. This time, however, they also examined the correlations between their findings and three city-level contextual variables – the total population of the cities in which the participants lived, the rates of violent crime for those cities, and the black population size for each city. Based on their ANOVA analyses, Correll and colleagues found support for both of their hypotheses. That is, they found that both their civilian participants and the two groups of police officers were more likely to incorrectly choose to "shoot" non-threatening blacks than non-threatening whites. They also found that the police officers were less likely to make mistakes than were their civilian participants. Finally, based on their correlational analyses, Correll and colleagues concluded that the mean level of incorrect "shootings" of blacks was related to residence in larger cities, cities with higher violent crime rates, and cities with larger black populations.[13]

Through their examination of both civilians' and police officers' decisions to shoot in their computer simulation game, as well as their

[13] Correll and colleagues' research therefore also supports criminal threat theories. For more details on how criminal threat theories applied to this study, see the review in the next section of this chapter.

correlational analysis of city-level context, Correll and colleagues most recent study provides relatively stronger support for a social threat theoretical framework than their two previous studies. In spite of their improvements, however, their study could still be improved methodologically by drawing random samples of police officer participants to reduce the potential for selection effects (i.e., certain types of police officers being more willing to participate in studies on the use of force). Additionally, by conducting multivariate regression analyses, instead of simple correlational analyses, Correll and colleagues might have more accurately determined how all participants' decision to "shoot" might have been influenced not only by race, but by a host of other control factors as well. Notwithstanding all of the methodological shortcomings of each of the simulation studies reviewed here, such studies provide some compelling, albeit suggestive only, support for racial/ethnic component of social threat theories of police use of force.

Other than the simulation studies reviewed above, there has been only one other individual-level, theory-driven, study of police use of force that has provided support for social threat theories in the past 20 years. Worden (1996) conducted a police officer-civilian encounter-based analysis of police officers' use of excessive force. He utilized systematic observational data of police-civilian encounters from the 1977 Police Services Study (PSS). In the PSS, trained observers accompanied police officers on 900 patrol shifts across 24 police departments in three metropolitan areas (Rochester, New York, St. Louis, Missouri, and the Tampa-St. Petersburg, Florida, area). During those 900 shifts, observers recorded 5,688 police officer-civilian encounters, of which police officers used excessive force in approximately 74 times (1.3% of all encounters). Then, based on Black's theory of law (Black 1976)[14], Worden hypothesized that

---

[14] Briefly, while Black's theory of law (1976) can most certainly be categorized as a social threat theory, the fit might not be as readily apparent to some. Instead of explaining which groups within a society should receive the most formal social control efforts due to their potential threat to the societal status hierarchy like most social threat theories, Black's theory seeks to explain why those same groups have less capacity to get the law to work in their favor (e.g., obtaining justice against police officers who use excessive force) than majority

racial/ethnic minorities would be more likely to experience excessive use of force by the police.

After conducting both bivariate and multivariate logistic regression analyses, Worden determined that black civilians had greater odds of experiencing the use of excessive force by the police than whites, net of a number of controls, including civilians' mental condition (i.e., signs of inebriation or mental illness), the carrying of a weapon, physically resisting police directions, and having a negative demeanor toward the officers. Based on these results, he concluded that "officers are, on average, more likely to adopt a punitive or coercive approach to black suspects than they are to white suspects" (37), thereby supporting the arguments made by social threat theorists. In addition to a more rigorous methodological approach, Worden was the first researcher to demonstrate that actual police officers were more likely to use force on racial/ethnic minorities in real-life encounters (in comparison to the computer simulation studies reviewed above). Subsequently, Worden's research provides relatively stronger and much more internally and externally valid support for the social threat theoretical framework at the individual-level.

The last empirical test of an individual-level social threat theory reviewed here is the only theory-driven study in the last twenty years to find no relationship between race and police use of force. A few years before the simulation studies reviewed earlier became popular, Dwyer and colleagues (Dwyer et al. 1990) conducted a simple analysis of 60 crime scene vignettes to assess how police officers responded to a variety of individual and situational characteristics, including suspect's race/ethnicity. They enlisted 142 officers from the Shelby County Sheriff's Office (Memphis, Tennessee) to voluntarily participate in

---

groups. Then, as a result of their being less able to have the law work toward their advantage, some groups effectively become more suitable targets for police abuses of force. However, because Black argues that it is primarily racial/ethnic minorities and lower social class individuals (he also mentions women) who have the least amount of access to the law, for by and large the same reasons that other social threat theories describe – it is those groups that represent the greatest threat to the status quo – his theory no doubt belongs right alongside each of the other theories/hypotheses discussed in this section.

their study (officers received no compensation). Each officer was given a booklet with 60 crime scene vignettes and was asked to decide whether they would 1) not draw their weapon, 2) draw, but not aim or fire their weapon, 3) draw and aim their weapon, but not fire it, or 4) draw their weapon, aim it, and shoot the suspect in the vignette. Across the vignettes a number of factors were manipulated, including the suspect's race (white vs. non-white). Based on what they referred to as "social script theory" (similar to the racial response bias argument made by Correll and colleagues [Correll et al. 2002; Correll et al. 2006; Correll et al. 2007]), Dwyer and colleagues hypothesized that the officers would be more likely to choose to shoot black suspects because of negative social scripts typically associated with racial/ethnic minorities in our society (1990).

In order to test their hypotheses, Dwyer and colleagues conducted multivariate OLS regression analyses. Quite unexpectedly to the researchers, they found that suspects' race *was not* related to officers' decisions to "shoot their weapon," even at a relaxed level of significance ($p > 0.25$). Unlike the simulation studies reviewed earlier, Dwyer and colleagues therefore concluded that police officers were no more likely to use force on non-whites than on whites. Unfortunately, however, due to the nature of their method, it is unlikely that the researchers were truly able to assess any automatic (subconscious) biases that might have affected the officers' decisions to shoot. That is, since the participants were able to take their time to choose their response – rather than being required to respond quickly to a computer simulation – the officers could have simply given the response they thought was more socially desirable or politically correct (i.e., making the decision regardless of race). So, where the simulation studies were specifically designed by psychologists to assess subconscious bias against racial/ethnic minorities, it is highly unlikely that Dwyer and colleagues' method was able to do the same, given the circumstances of their study. Consequently, as theirs was the only theory-driven test of social threat theories to find no significant relationship between race and police officers' decisions to use force, the viability of a social threat theoretical framework should not seriously be called into question.

Overall, based on the aggregate- and individual-level empirical tests reviewed above, the social threat theoretical framework appears to be an adequate, if not strong, explanation for all forms of police use of force. Table 2.1, presented at the end of this chapter, displays condensed summaries of each of the studies reviewed here. Reported in the table are the specific aggregate- and individual-level theories or hypotheses that were tested, the data and methods that were used (when reported), and the major findings of each study. In general, as most of the aggregate-level tests revealed, measures of race/ethnicity appear to be much better predictors of rates of police use of force than are measures of social class (i.e. income inequality). An interesting consequence of these findings is the need for research on *why* threats from lower social class groups are not met with as much police use of force as threats from racial/ethnic minorities. Have changes in the economic structure of the U.S. affected how the level of threat presented by lower social class groups is perceived by the powerful elites? Or, perhaps, the demographic composition of the U.S. has changed enough to make racial/ethnic minority groups even more threatening (the U.S. Census Bureau recently announced that the U.S. will become a "majority minority" nation by 2050 [U.S. Census Bureau 2008])? Future research that examines how the powerful groups in our society perceive threat may help us answer such questions.

In addition to the finding that lower social class groups may not present as much of a social threat as once thought, the general consensus of the studies reviewed above was that blacks are much more likely to be the recipients of police use of force, not only compared to whites, but also compared to other racial/ethnic minorities. Thus, based on both the aggregate- and individual-level research, it appears that blacks are perceived to present the greatest social threat to the powerful groups in our society. However, with the recent increases in the U.S. Hispanic population, it should be interesting to learn whether or not Hispanics begin, or already have begun, experiencing similarly high levels of police use of force. Is there a threshold at which the relative size of a racial/ethnic minority group begins to present enough of a social threat that the group's members also begin to experience more formal social control? In order to determine if such a threshold exists, future research should continue to examine how different racial/ethnic minorities differentially experience police use of force. Regardless of what future research may show, however, social threat theories of police use of force have, to date, received empirical support at both the aggregate- and individual-levels.

Criminal Threat Theories

Criminal threat theories generally contend that police officers use force in response to threatening individuals, situations, and environments (or what they *perceive* to be threatening). So, rather than viewing police use of force as an tool for controlling groups or individuals who pose a social threat to the powerful groups in our society, criminal threat theories posit that police officers will use force on anyone, powerful or powerless, that poses a criminal threat (i.e., a threat of physical harm) to their own safety, the safety of their fellow officers, or the safety of the general public. Among the theories and hypotheses included under the broader heading of the criminal threat theoretical framework are the danger perception theory (Fyfe 1980; MacDonald, Kaminski, Alpert, and Tennenbaum 2001; MacDonald, Alpert, and Tennenbaum 1999; Sherman and Langworthy 1979), community threat or community violence theories (Holmes, Reynolds, Holmes, and Faulkner 1998; Kania and Mackey 1977; Sorenson et al. 1993), and what have been generally referred to as threatening acts hypotheses (Holmes 2000; Liska and Yu 1992; Smith and Holmes 2003; Worden 1996).

MacDonald and colleagues (2001) best described the general criminal threat argument by describing not only how real, physical, and immediate threats were related to police officers' use of force, but also how *perceived* threats might also influence officers' use of force. They asserted that "the level of police use of deadly force is contingent on the danger police officers experience (real or perceived) . . . [and that] police officers are more likely to use deadly force during time periods when (or in places where) they encounter greater levels of violence or *view their jobs as being particularly hazardous*" (159, emphasis added). And, even though MacDonald and his colleagues were referring specifically to deadly forms of police force, the danger-perception theory they used, and criminal threat theories in general, all contend that police officers should be more likely to use all types of force (legitimate and illegitimate, lethal and non-lethal) when they receive direct threats to their own safety (e.g., when dealing with an armed criminal suspect), or when they perceive a potential threat to their, or someone else's, safety (e.g., when working in an area with high levels of criminal activity).

Empirical Tests of Criminal Threat Theories

Empirical tests of criminal threat theories have used a variety of measures that assess criminal activity at the aggregate-level, and criminal dangerousness at the individual-level. Among the aggregate-level measures that are most commonly used in the literature are rates of public violence (i.e., riots and violent protests), rates of homicides or other crimes, and even rates of arrest. At the individual-level, criminal threat measures often include individuals' aggressive and violent behaviors toward police officers (i.e., resisting arrest or physically assaulting an officer), the presence and/or displaying of a weapon, and the individual's mental state (i.e., being mental ill or being under the influence of a controlled substance). Using these measures, criminal threat theorists expect that both aggregate-level rates of criminal activity and individual-level measures of dangerousness should be positively related to police use of force behaviors. Not surprisingly, the majority of researchers who have conducted empirical tests of criminal threat theories have found just that.

Historically (again referring to those studies conducted more than 20 years ago), aggregate-level research has consistently shown that areas with high rates of criminal activity also tend to have high rates of police use of force (e.g., Binder and Scharf 1982; Fyfe 1980; Jacobs and Britt 1979; Kania and Mackey 1977; Sherman and Langworthy 1979; Sherman 1986). Similarly, individual-level tests have found that police officers who dealt with more real or perceived criminals, violence, and dangerous crimes in general were significantly more likely to use force (e.g., Binder and Fridell 1984; Binder and Scharf 1982; Copeland 1986; Horvath 1987). Traditionally, then, there has strong support for criminal threat theories of police officers' use of force. More recent empirical tests have been just as consistently supportive.

Aggregate-Level Evidence

MacDonald and colleagues (MacDonald et al. 1999) were the first researchers to consider how aggregate-level rates of crime temporally corresponded with rates of police use of force. In particular, they examined how high rates of homicide across the nation covaried with high rates of police use of deadly force over time. They used national homicide data from the FBI's SHR for every month between the years 1976 and 1986 to conduct their study. Based on the danger perception theory, they created a "reactive hypothesis" which argued that increases in rates of certain types of homicides would cause police to perceive higher levels of danger in their jobs, which would subsequently lead to higher rates of police officers' use of deadly force in the same month that the homicide rates spiked. Specifically, they believed that police officers would be most likely to react with deadly force when rates of robbery-related and justifiable civilian homicides (i.e., when a civilian uses deadly force to protect him or herself or loved ones) were high because the circumstances of those types of homicides are also strong indicators of potentially dangerous situations to which police officers might have to respond.

In order to test their hypotheses, MacDonald and colleagues conducted an autoregressive integrated moving average (ARIMA) time series analysis that allowed them to control for the high level of temporal autocorrelation across their 132 months of homicide data. The results of their analyses revealed that during months in which both the rates of robbery-related and justifiable civilian homicides were high, the rates of police officers' use of deadly force were also high. Subsequently, the researchers concluded that "the incidence of police use of deadly force closely follow[ed] the dangerousness of particular time periods" (162). Such evidence strongly supports the criminal threat theoretical framework. Unfortunately, however, while MacDonald and colleagues' research was methodologically sound, they failed to include any potentially confounding measures in their ARIMA models to control for the possibility of an alternative explanation(s) for their results. So, even though MacDonald and colleagues were able to demonstrate a strong temporal relationship between crime rates and police officers' use of deadly force, even they acknowledged that further research was necessary that included not only a variety of covariate control measures, but research that also attempted to predict forms of police behaviors other than the use of deadly force.

In a follow-up to their earlier study, MacDonald and colleagues (2001) reexamined how national homicide rates affected rates of police use of deadly force over time. This time, however, they expanded the time frame of their analysis to include 21 years (1976 – 1996), and conducted additional stationarity tests to make sure that their findings were as reliable as possible. Monthly homicide data, including their dependent variable (police officers' use of deadly force) once again came from the FBI's SHR. As with their earlier study, they employed the danger-perception theory to propose another "reactive hypothesis," in which they argued that increases in robbery-related and justifiable civilian homicides would be related to increases in police officers' use of excessive force.

In an effort to increase the reliability of their estimates this time around, MacDonald and colleagues not only conducted another set of ARIMA time series analyses, they also conducted several stationarity tests. These stationarity tests allowed them to determine whether the processes driving the temporal relationships between their homicide rate measures and police use of deadly force measure were invariant over time (i.e., stationary), or if those processes changed over time (i.e., non-stationary). Had their tests revealed that the relationships were non-stationary, MacDonald and colleagues would be unable to definitively conclude that some other unmeasured temporal covariate had not influenced both their independent and dependent measures (i.e., the relationships were spurious). Fortunately, the results of their stationarity tests indicated that the relationships they observed were indeed stationary over time, lending added support to their substantive findings. And, as they had observed in their earlier study, MacDonald and colleagues once again found that periods of time which had higher rates of robbery-related and justifiable civilian homicides also tended to have higher rates of police use of deadly force.

As a result of the two separate studies described above, MacDonald and colleagues provided some of the strongest support for the criminal threat theoretical framework. Moreover, in their more recent study (MacDonald et al. 2001), because the researchers were also able to improve their methodology, they were able to obtain more reliable findings as well. Unfortunately, however, while their stationarity tests revealed that the relationship that they had observed was not spurious, they still failed to include any other covariates in their models to control for alternative explanations of changes in police use of deadly force over time. Furthermore, because both of the studies by MacDonald and colleagues focused exclusively on police officers' use of deadly force, the propensity of criminal threat theories for explaining non-lethal police use of force is still unclear.

Fortunately, other research has shown that criminal threat measures are capable of not only explaining other, non-lethal forms of police use of force, but that they are also robust to the inclusion of a variety of control variables.   In another recent study in which MacDonald also took part, Alpert and MacDonald (2001) found that violent crime rates positively and significantly predicted police officers' use of all types of force (i.e., both lethal and non-lethal). Data for the researchers' study came from an unidentified national PERF survey of law enforcement agencies that took place in 1998. A total of 265 agencies provided official data on police use of force incidents during the 1996 calendar year, which Alpert and MacDonald then used to calculate rates of police use of force per 100,000 individuals in the areas served by each agency.   The violent crime rates for those areas served as the primary measure of aggregate-level criminal threat. Based on a general criminal threat argument (they cited both the "reactive hypothesis" utilized in MacDonald and colleagues' earlier studies [1999; 2001] and the "community violence hypothesis" that other researchers have used [e.g., Sorensen et al. 1993]), Alpert and MacDonald hypothesized that areas with high rates of violent crime would also have high rates of police use of *all types* of force.

To test their hypothesis, Alpert and MacDonald (2001) conducted basic bivariate and multivariate OLS regression analyses. In order to account for the skewed distribution of their police use of force dependent variable (toward zero), they calculated its natural log for use in their analyses (see Jacobs and O'Brien [1998] for precedent). The results of their bivariate analyses revealed that increases in the rates of violent crime were strongly associated with increases in police use of all types of physical force. Alpert and MacDonald then also found that their violent crime rate measure was the strongest predictor of police use of force of all the covariates included in their multivariate analysis. Subsequently, as a result of their focus of all forms of police use of force, and due to their inclusion of a variety of control measures, Alpert and MacDonald's results are not only more generalizable and robust than MacDonald's previous research, they also provide even more evidence in support of a criminal threat theoretical framework of police use of force.

In addition to the research conducted by the above researchers, the inherent logic of criminal threat theories has not escaped those who fall under the banner of "social threat theorists." As such, many of the theory-driven empirical tests of criminal threat theories at both the aggregate- and individual-levels have also included at least one measure of criminal threat. It should therefore be unsurprising that all five of the aggregate-level social threat studies that were reviewed above included measures of criminal threat and accordingly proposed and tested a variety of criminal threat theories as well (Holmes 2000; Jacobs and O'Brien 1998; Liska and Yu; Smith and Holmes 2003; Sorensen et al. 1993). To conserve space, those studies are not reviewed again in specific detail. Instead, only the researchers' measure(s) of criminal threat, the specific criminal threat theories guiding their hypotheses, and their findings as they relate to the broader criminal threat theoretical framework are reviewed below.

Jacobs and O'Brien (1998) used city-level rates of homicides obtained from the FBI's UCR as their measure of criminal threat in order to test the same "reactive hypothesis" that MacDonald and colleagues (1999; 2001) utilized. Specifically, they hypothesized that the rates of homicides in cities across the nation would be positively related to rates of police use of deadly force (FBI's SHR). The results of their Tobit analyses revealed that homicide rates indeed predicted police officers' use of deadly force, net of the social threat measures that they had also found to be related to rates of police use of deadly force. Consequently, because their study was one of the more methodologically sound empirical analyses of police officers' use of force, Jacobs and O'Brien's findings not only provide very strong evidence in support of social threat theories, but very strong in support of criminal threat theories as well.

Sorensen and colleagues' (1993) used city-level violent crime rates (i.e., rates of homicide, rape, robbery, and aggravated assault) obtained from the FBI's UCR to test what they referred to as the "community violence" hypothesis. They expected that increases in violent crime rates would increase the level of dangerousness perceived by police officers, which in turn would result in increased rates of police use of deadly force (FBI's SHR). The results of Sorensen and colleagues' OLS regression analyses revealed that rates of violent crime significantly predicted rates of police officers' use of deadly force, net of their social threat measures, just as Jacobs and O'Brien (1998) had observed. Furthermore, they found that city-level violent crime rates were the strongest predictors of police use of deadly force in each of their models. Thus, even though Sorensen and colleagues' study was not as methodologically sound as Jacobs and O'Brien's study (see review above), it does provide some additional support for the criminal threat theoretical framework of police use of force.

Like their counterparts, Liska and Yu (1992) found support for criminal threat theories as well. They utilized three measures of criminal threat, all of which were obtained from the FBI's UCR: 1) the overall rate of all Index I crimes (homicide/non-negligent manslaughter, rape, robbery, aggravated assault, larceny, burglary, automobile theft, and arson), 2) the rates of violent crimes only (the first four index crimes listed previously), and 3) the rates of homicides on their own. Based on what the researchers referred to as "the threatening acts theory," they hypothesized that all three measures would be positively related to rates of police use of deadly force (FBI's SHR).

The results of Liska and Yu's structural-measurement models revealed that homicide rates on their own were the only significantly predictors of police use of deadly force, but that it had one of the strongest effects. However, because the researchers included three crime rate measures simultaneously, it is not be surprising that the one measure of criminal threat that is the most likely to be perceived as especially dangerous to police officers (i.e., the homicide rate) was also the only measure to significantly predict rates of their use of deadly force. Thus, like the two previous studies of police use of deadly force (Jacobs and O'Brien 1998; Sorensen et al. 1993), Liska and Yu's research provides further support for criminal threat theories.

The final two aggregate studies from the past 20 years that empirically tested both social threat and criminal threat theories were Holmes' (2000) and Smith and Holmes' (2003) examinations of civilian complaints of police use of excessive force. Because the latter study was a replication of the former, and because they utilized the same criminal threat measures to obtain the same results, they are reviewed in concert. For each study, the researchers followed Liska and Yu's (1992) lead and used the same Index I crime rate measure (FBI's UCR) and the same "threatening acts theory" as the basis for their research.

Unexpectedly, however, the researchers found no significant relationship between the Index I crime rates and civilian complaints of police use of excessive force in either study. Given Liska and Yu's (1992) earlier findings, one possible explanation for the researchers' null findings becomes apparent. While Liska and Yu found that overall Index I crime rates were not significantly related to police officers' use of deadly force, they did find that homicide rates alone significantly predicted variation in their outcome variable. Subsequently, it appears that homicide rates on their own (i.e., not when combined with other types of crime rates) are the best predictors of police officers perceptions of criminal threat. Despite their null findings then, the two pieces by Holmes (2000) and Smith and Holmes (2003) help to shed light on just how police officers perceive criminal threats differently for different types of crime. Overall then, the aggregate-level evidence in support of a criminal threat theoretical framework of police use of force is still quite strong.

Individual-Level Evidence

Individual-level criminal threat theories generally contend that police officers will be more likely to use any and all types of force when they perceive a direct threat of physical harm against their own well-being or the well-being of others (i.e., fellow police officers or civilian bystanders). Accordingly, rather than studying how rates of crime influence rates of police use of force, individual-level tests of the criminal threat theoretical framework typically examine how police officers use force during specific encounters with criminals or other potentially dangerous individuals (i.e., mentally unstable individuals or those under the influence of controlled substances).

Holmes, Reynolds, Holmes, and Faulkner (1998) examined a number of factors that might influence how police officers perceive criminal threat. While the researchers did not attempt empirically test any predictors of actual police use of force behaviors, Holmes and colleagues' research helps shed light on the aspects of a police officer-civilian/criminal encounter that may lead police officers to perceive a threat and then use force to either prevent the escalation of the situation or to gain control of the situation once it has already become dangerous. In order to determine what aspects of an encounter might lead police officers to use force, the researchers therefore conducted a survey of 662 sworn police officers from the London, Ohio, police training academy. In the survey, police cadets were presented with a number of fictional vignettes describing a variety of potentially threatening scenarios. Holmes and colleagues then asked the officers to decide whether the circumstances described in each vignette were threatening enough to necessitate the use of force. Based on what they called a "threat presentation" hypothesis, the researchers expected that officers would be more likely to perceive a threat which necessitated the use of force when the characters in the vignette were 1) mentally or emotionally unstable, 2) suspected of committing a serious crime, or 3) physically resisting arrest.

Unfortunately, Holmes and colleagues (1998) do not clearly specify the analytic technique they used to test their hypotheses, but based on the presentation of their results, it appears that they conducted a number of multivariate OLS regression analyses. Whatever their actual analytic strategy, the researchers found that the scenarios in which the fictional characters resisted arrest were the most likely to lead officers to perceive a threat serious enough for them to use force. Scenarios in which the characters had committed a more serious crime also caused officers to perceive enough threat to use force. Surprisingly, however, in the scenarios where the officers encountered mentally or emotionally unstable individuals, the officers reported that there was not a strong or immediate enough of a threat that they felt the need to use force. Overall, Holmes and colleagues' research provides some initial support for a criminal threat theoretical framework for explaining police use of force, but because they do not examine police officers' actual use of force behaviors (and, to a lesser extent, because their methods are unclear), no definitive conclusions can, or should, be drawn based upon their findings.

Somewhat surprisingly, Holmes and colleagues' study was the only individual-level research in the last twenty years that exclusively tested a criminal threat theory. Rather, nearly all of the empirical tests of individual-level criminal threat theories are found in the studies testing the social threat theoretical framework reviewed above. To conserve space once again, the data and methods of those studies are not reviewed in detail. Instead, only the researchers' measure(s) of criminal threat, the specific criminal threat theories guiding their hypotheses, and their findings as they relate to support for criminal threat theories are reviewed below.

In each of the four simulation studies reviewed earlier in this chapter (Correll et al. 2002; Correll et al. 2006; Correll et al. 2007; Greenwald et al. 2003), the researchers presented their participants with images not only of individuals of different racial/ethnic backgrounds, but also images of individuals with either weapons or some other non-weapon items in their hands (e.g., bottles, cell-phones, wallets, etc.). Based on the threatening acts theory, the researchers all hypothesized that their participants (both civilians and police officers) would be more likely to correctly and more quickly choose to "shoot" images of individuals holding weapons in comparison to individuals holding the other non-weapon items. Not surprisingly, the researchers each independently observed that their civilian participants were more likely to make more correct decisions faster when they were presented with images of individuals holding weapons (Correll et al. 2002; Correll et al. 2006; Greenwald et al. 2003), although police officers responded more quickly and were correct more often in comparison to their civilian counterparts (Correll et al. 2007). Subsequently, the results of all four simulation studies are strongly supportive of not only the social threat theoretical framework, but criminal threat framework as well.

The only other empirical test of both social threat and criminal threat theories over the past 20 years was Worden's (1996) study of police officers' use of excessive force. Unlike the studies reviewed above, Worden utilized systematic observational data from the PSS. He was subsequently able to test how criminal suspects' *actual behaviors* influenced police officers' use of force (as compared to the behaviors of the digitized "suspects" used in the simulation studies above). Once again employing the threatening acts theory used by other researchers, Worden hypothesized that suspects who physically resisted arrest, or who tried to attack officers, would have greater odds of having excessive levels of force used against them. As expected, the results of his logistic regression analyses revealed that those suspects whose actions toward police officers were threatening (i.e., who resisted or tried to attack) had greater odds of experiencing police use of excessive force, net of a variety of other control measures, including all of the social threat measures described earlier in this chapter. As a result, Worden's study helps to substantiate the findings of the simulation studies reviewed above, and provides more evidence that criminal threat at the individual-level is indeed a strong explanation of police officers' use of force.

All together, the aggregate- and individual-level empirical tests reviewed above strongly suggest that the criminal threat theoretical framework is not only a viable explanation for police officers' use of force, but a very powerful one as well. Table 2.1 below presents brief summaries of each of the studies reviewed above that empirically tested a criminal threat theory. Again, for each study, the table displays the specific criminal threat theory that drove the researchers' analyses, the data and methods that were utilized (when reported), and the most important findings that were observed. In general, however, there are three broad conclusions that can be drawn from the criminal threat literature as a whole.

First, in many of the studies that tested both social threat and criminal theories, the measures of criminal threat were usually the strongest predictors of the various measures of police officers' use of force. Although a couple studies found no significant effects of criminal threat measures when controlling for social threat measures (Holmes 2000; Smith and Holmes 2003), the majority of researchers found that their measures of criminal threat predicted police officers' use of force better than their measures of social threat. Upon further consideration, however, this general finding should not be surprising given that criminal threats are more likely to have an immediate and potentially dangerous impact on police officers' well-being than are social threats, which may not directly affect police officers at all. Furthermore, police officers are legally justified to use of force when they (or others) are physically threatened (i.e., presented with a criminal threat), but are not legally justified to use force when they (or others) are threatened socially.

Given these considerations, future research should therefore continue to simultaneously test both theoretical frameworks to further disentangle the direct and indirect relationships between social threat measures, criminal threat measures, and police officers' use of force. For example, does the social threat that racial/ethnic minorities present lead to them be viewed as more of a criminal threat as well? Do any other behavioral (e.g., disrespect, verbal resistance, fleeing, etc.) factors influence police officers' perceptions of criminal threat? What about other factors not related to an individual's behavior (e.g., age, gender, appearance, etc.)? Answers to such questions may help us better understand the processes which lead police officers to use force.

Second, based on some of the aggregate-level studies reviewed above, it appears that homicide rates may be much better indicators of criminal threat than other rates of crime. This suggests that police officers are most likely to use force when they perceive more serious or significant criminal threats. Future research should therefore explore how the threat associated with different types of crimes influence police officers' use of force behaviors. If the overall homicide rate truly is the best predictor of police use of force because it leads officers to be more concerned about their own well-being, what effect might rates of assaults on police officers, or rates of homicides of police officers, have on their use of force behavior? In areas where rates of assaults and homicides of police officers are high, will officers be more likely to use force to preempt more attacks? Will they use more force in retaliation against the attacks on their fellow officers? Future research should consider these questions so that we may better understand how police officers' perceive and respond to different kinds of criminal threats.

Finally, while a number of the aggregate-level tests of the criminal threat theoretical framework have demonstrated that crime rates can influence rates of police use of force, the majority of the theory-driven research at the individual-level has come from simulation studies. It is important to note that there have also been a number of *non-theory-driven* studies at the individual- or encounter-level that have nonetheless included typical measures of criminal threat (e.g., resisting arrest and assaulting officers) that find that police officers are more likely to use force when threatened (e.g., Garner et al. 2002). Unfortunately, in those studies, the researchers simply included as many variables in their analyses as they had available to them, with no theoretical expectations for what they might observe. Consequently, it is difficult to interpret their results in terms of theory. More individual-level, theory-driven, empirical tests of criminal threat theories that utilize other forms of data (i.e., other than simulation and observational studies) are needed to determine exactly how and why police officers respond to criminal threats in the ways that they do.

Klinger's Ecological Theory of Police Vigor

Klinger's (1997) ecological theory of police vigor is the only new theory of police behavior that has been proposed in recent years. While his theory was not specifically intended to explain police use of force, based on the theoretical arguments he makes, it would be relatively easy to empirically determine whether or not his theory constitutes a third viable theoretical explanation of police use of force. In this section, Klinger's theory is reviewed and discussed in regards to how it might be adapted to explain police use of force behaviors.

In 1997, Klinger proposed his "ecological theory of police response to deviance." His primary argument in this theory was that the amount of vigor police officers used to do their jobs should be related to the ecological contexts in which they work. In other words, he believed that the environments that police officers worked in on a day-to-day basis might influence the amount of energy, effort, or desire that officers put into completing their duties. Specifically, he contended that four problems affecting police vigor would arise as a result of police officers working in high crime areas: 1) an increased tolerance for deviant and criminal behavior, 2) decreased perceptions of crime victims' deservingness, 3) increased levels of cynicism toward the value of their crime-fighting efforts, and 4) the increased size of their workloads. Each problem is discussed in more detail below.

First, Klinger argued that officers would put less vigor into the execution of their duties when they believed that the residents within their patrol beats were tolerant, if not accepting, of deviant and criminal behaviors. Essentially, he believed that after working in areas where residents had become desensitized to deviance and/or crime, police officers might also become desensitized such behaviors and consequently use less vigor responding to, or attempting to prevent, said problems since they no longer considered those behaviors to be as serious as an objective outsider might. For example, if an officer

Table 2.1. Theory-Driven Studies of Police Use of Force During the Last 20 Years

Aggregate-Level Studies

Author(s)	Data	Method(s)	Specific Theory Tested	Significant Findings
Alpert & MacDonald (2001)	Unidentified Police Executive Research Forum Study	OLS Regression	Reactive/Community Violence (CT)	Violent Crime Rate → (+) / **Rates of Police Use of Force**
Holmes (2000)	Police Brutality Study; U.S. Census Report; Uniform Crime Report	Poisson-Based OLS Regression	Minority Threat (ST); Threatening Acts (CT)	Percent Black → (+) / Percent Hispanic → (+) / Racial Income Inequality → (+) / **Rates of Police Use of Excessive Force**
Jacobs & O'Brien (1998)	Supplementary Homicides Report; U.S. Census Report; Uniform Crime Report	Tobit Regression	Political Threat (ST); Reactive (CT)	Racial Income Inequality → (+) / Percent Black → (+) / Homicide Rates → (+) / **Rates of Police Use of Deadly Force**
Liska & Yu (1992)	Vital Statistics; U.S. Census Report; Uniform Crime Report	Structural Measurement Models	Threat (ST); Threatening Acts (CT)	Percent Non-White → (+) / Racial Segregation → (+) / Homicide Rate → (+) / **Rates of Police Use of Deadly Force**
MacDonald, Alpert, & Tennenbaum (1999)	Supplementary Homicides Report	Autoregressive Integrated Moving Average Time Series	Danger Perception (CT)	Robbery-Related Homicide Rate → (+) / Justifiable Civilian Homicide Rate → (+) / **Rates of Police Use of Deadly Force**
MacDonald, Kaminski, Alpert, & Tennenbaum (2001)	Supplementary Homicides Report	Autoregressive Integrated Moving Average Time Series; Stationarity Tests	Danger Perception (CT)	Robbery-Related Homicide Rate → (+) / Justifiable Civilian Homicide Rate → (+) / **Rates of Police Use of Deadly Force**
Smith & Holmes (2003)	Police Brutality Study; U.S. Census Report; Uniform Crime Report	Negative Binomial Regression	Minority Threat (ST); Threatening Acts (CT)	Percent Black → (+) / Percent Hispanic → (+) / **Rates of Police Use of Excessive Force**
Sorensen, Marquart, and Brock (1993)	Supplementary Homicides Report; U.S. Census Report; Uniform Crime Report	OLS Regression	Conflict (ST); Community Violence (CT)	Percent Black → (+) / Percent in Poverty → (+) / Income Inequality → (+) / Violent Crime Rate → (+) / **Rates of Police Use of Deadly Force**

Notes: CT = Criminal Threat; ST = Social Threat

Table 2.1. Theory-Driven Studies of Police Use of Force During the Last 20 Years, Contd.

Individual-Level Studies

Author(s)	Data	Method(s)	Specific Theory Tested	Significant Findings
Correll, Park, Judd, & Wittenbrink (2002)	University of Colorado	Analysis of Variance	Racial Response Bias (ST); Threatening Acts (CT)	Black Suspect → (+) Presence of a Weapon → (+) **Decision to Use Deadly Force**
Correll, Park, Judd, Wittenbrink, Sadler, and Keesee (2007)	Denver (Colorado) Department of Motor Vehicles; Denver Police Department; Denver Police Training Seminar	Analysis of Variance; Correlational	Racial Response Bias (ST); Threatening Acts (CT)	Black Suspect → (+) Presence of a Weapon → (+) **Decision to Use Deadly Force**
Correll, Urland, & Ito (2006)	University of Colorado	Analysis of Variance	Racial Response Bias (ST); Threatening Acts (CT)	Black Suspect → (+) Presence of a Weapon → (+) **Decision to Use Deadly Force**
Dwyer, Graesser, Hopkinson, & Lupfer (1990)	Shelby County (Tennessee); Sheriff's Office	OLS Regression	Social Script (ST)	No Significant Results
Greenwald, Oakes, & Hoffman (2003)	University of Washington	Unidentified	Racial Response Bias (ST); Threatening Acts (CT)	Black Suspect → (+) **Decision to Use Force**
Holmes, Reynolds, Holmes, & Faulkner (1998)	London (Ohio) Police Department	Unidentified	Threat Presentation (CT)	Physical Resistance → (+) Seriousness of Offense → (+) **Police Decision to Use Force**
Worden (1996)	Police Services Study	Logistic Regression	Black's Theory of Law (ST); Threatening Acts (CT)	Black Suspect → (+) Physical Resistance → (+) Assault Officer → (+) **Police Use of Excessive Force**

Notes: CT = Criminal Threat; ST = Social Threat

worked in an area where prostitution and drug dealing were tolerated, if not accepted by residents, Klinger argued that police officers might also become tolerant of those behaviors and, as a result, put less effort into enforcing the laws regulating those criminal behaviors. Thus, in high crime areas, police officers might use less vigor because they no longer view certain deviant or criminal behaviors as being unworthy of their time and energy.

Second, Klinger contended that police officers may also use less vigor when they perceive the victims of criminal offenses to be undeserving of their attention or efforts. Specifically, he argued that in areas with high levels of crime, police officers might often deal with crime victims who had helped precipitate their own victimization. For example, if officers responded to a lot of calls where an individual was assaulted or robbed while he or she was under the influence of some illicit substance, Klinger believed that those officers might then start blaming the victim for bringing about their own victimization. That is, if the victim had not been under the influence of an illegal substance in the first place, they would not have been an easier target for being assaulted or robbed in the first place. So, because some victims may help to create the environment that leads to their victimization, Klinger believed that some officers might be less sympathetic to those victims' plights. Subsequently, if police officers were forced to handle a large number of incidents in which the crime victim was not wholly without fault, then Klinger argued that police officers would begin to view those victims as being less worthy of their efforts.

Third, Klinger posited that neighborhoods with high levels of crime may lead the officers working in those neighborhoods to become jaded to the extent that they might even believe that their no matter their vigor, all their efforts to fight crime were futile. In other words, if police officers did their best day-in and day-out to fight crime, but nevertheless continued to see the issues persist despite all of their hard work, Klinger believed that those officers would start becoming cynical about the prospect of their ever really having a chance to be successful. In turn, the officers' cynical attitudes toward the value of their work might then lead to them to put less effort into actually fulfilling their duties. Thus, Klinger expected that in areas where rates of crime had been high for long periods of time, despite police officers' best efforts to control such behaviors, they would become less likely to put forth such effort in the future.

Finally, Klinger suggested that because police officers working in high crime areas often had more crimes with which they had to deal, they also had deal with much heavier workloads. These heavier workloads, he argued, would eventually lead to officers becoming overwhelmed with all the related paperwork, follow-up investigations, and court appearances associated with making many arrests. Subsequently, Klinger believed that those overworked officers might start putting less effort into their jobs, so they might once again find balance in their lives. Then, if those officers' workloads eventually became smaller and more easily manageable due to their lack of vigor, they would then have even less cause (or inclination) to ever go back to fully performing their duties. Thus, Klinger expected that police officers working in high crime areas would use less vigor in the execution of their duties because less work increased the likelihood that they would be able to "get home on time every night."

<u>Klinger's Theory as an Explanation for Police Use of Force</u>

Although Klinger may not have originally intended for this ecological theory to be used as a theoretical framework for explaining police use of force, with some thoughtful interpretation, it has the potential to serve as another valuable tool for helping researchers understand both police vigor and use of force. Unfortunately, however, given the general conclusions of the empirical tests of the criminal threat theoretical framework and the lines of Klinger's original arguments, it is possible that researchers might follow two very different paths for explaining police officers' use of force.

First of all, given that the majority of the research testing criminal threat theories concluded that high crime rates were associated with increased rates of police use of force, it is reasonable to expect that the four problems associated with police vigor in high crime neighborhoods that Klinger originally identified (residents' tolerance of crime, the undeservingness of victims, police cynicism, and heavy workloads) might actually lead to more police use of force. That is, in addition to perceiving greater criminal threats in high-crime neighborhoods, those four problems might also lead police officers to use more force in order to "punish" the people that make their jobs more difficult. Consequently, one might use Klinger's theory to argue that police officers should use *more* force in high-crime areas.

Second, Klinger's ecological theory of police vigor could also be used to argue that police officers should use *less* force in high crime areas too, however. One simple argument for such an effect would simply be that because the use of force can often require a great deal of physical effort, less vigorous police officers should be less inclined to engage in such behaviors. In order to further illustrate how Klinger's theory might be used to explain reduced rates of police use of force in high-crime areas, however, it is useful to independently consider each of the four problems that he originally identified.

Beginning with Klinger's argument that the tolerance of criminal behavior in high-crime areas should decrease police officers' vigor, a compelling argument could be made that if those officers use less vigor in their duties, then they should have fewer encounters with criminals, and fewer encounters means fewer opportunities to use force. It also stands to reason that if police officers believe that crime victims are undeserving of their efforts, then those officers should also be less likely to use force during their investigations of possible suspects or in order to protect the undeserving victims. Next, if officers who worked in high-crime areas did become so cynical that they truly believed that their efforts had little or no effect crime, it would be unlikely that they would feel inclined use force, since doing so would also have very little affect on crime (at least, from those officers' perspective). Finally, as all police officers know, the use of force almost always necessitates a considerable amount of paperwork (i.e., filling out use-of-force reports). Subsequently, this may also cause police officers to use less force, even if they have more opportunities or justifications to do so, if only to avoid filling out more reports. Thus, as laid out above, Klinger's theory can not only be very easily adapted to explaining increased police use of force in high-crime areas, but decreased use of force in those same areas as well.

As a result of the two very different ways in which Klinger's ecological theory of police vigor can be adapted to explain police use of force, it may come down to an empirical test of the theory in order to determine which adaptation, if either, is most appropriate. And, while such a study is a promising direction for future research, the object of this book is not to test Klinger's theory as an explanation for police use of force, but to propose and test an alternative theory for how neighborhood context might affect police behavior. Subsequently, until an empirical test of an adapted version of Klinger's theory aimed at explaining police officers' use of force (such as the one outlined here) can be conducted, it is impossible to determine its true viability.

As a final note, while an adaptation of Klinger's theory is a good start, the general lack of theoretical frameworks for explaining police use of force (i.e., only the two reviewed above – social threat and criminal threat), as well as the lack of empirical tests of those frameworks, clearly indicates that more research is needed. As Table 2.1 above displays, there were only 15 empirical studies over the past 20 years that have utilized theory to drive their analyses. This is regrettable. If researchers do not use theory to help us understand how and why some factor influences police officers' use of force, it is that much more difficult to determine exactly how manipulating that factor might affect police officers' behaviors for better or worse. Consequently, in order to not only further our understanding of police officers' use of force, but also to improve our capacity as researchers to inform real-world policies regarding police actions, more theoretical frameworks must be developed and tested.

CHAPTER 3

The Influence of Neighborhoods on Crime

While the lack of theory in policing research is a significant issue that needs to be addressed, another important theme that needs to be considered, and which is conspicuous in its relative absence from the police use of force literature, is the influence of neighborhood context. As the object of this book is to establish a relationship between police officers' use of force behaviors and the contextual factors associated with the neighborhoods in which they work, this research should contribute to that gap in the literature. Before discussing exactly how neighborhood context is expected to influence police behavior, however, it is useful to review the existing research on neighborhoods and crime, which will be relied upon heavily for the theoretical arguments made later in this book (see Chapter 4) linking the social disorganization tradition to police officers' use of force.

Although the theory of social disorganization is commonly, and appropriately, attributed to Clifford Shaw and Henry McKay, what this research refers to as *the social disorganization tradition* can be attributed to a much larger body of researchers. For the purposes of this book, the social disorganization tradition can therefore be defined as the combination of both Shaw and McKay's original theory *and* the works of a number of later researchers who have each made significant modifications to the concept of neighborhood social disorganization. Accordingly, throughout the remainder of this book, whenever any neighborhood contextual concepts attributable to any of the various researchers discussed in this chapter are mentioned, they will be referred to as coming from *the social disorganization tradition*, rather than coming from any particular researcher or group of researchers.

The Origins of Social Disorganization

The theory of social disorganization is rooted in Clifford Shaw and Henry McKay's research on juvenile delinquency in Chicago, Illinois, during the 1920s and 1930s. Their theory, however, is founded in works of other researchers who came from what is commonly known as *the Chicago School*, of which both Shaw and McKay were later a part. The Chicago School refers to any of the research or researchers that came out of the University of Chicago's Department of Sociology (especially related to the discipline of Urban Sociology) during the first half of the 20th century.

The Chicago School has long considered how the neighborhoods in which individuals live could influence how they behave. Years before Shaw and McKay would conceive of their much more widely-recognized theory of social disorganization, however, another group of researchers from the Chicago School mapped out the growth of Chicago using concentric zones emanating outwards from the center of the city's downtown area. Park, Burgess, and McKenzie (1925) identified five concentric zones which not only had very different demographic, social, and economic compositions, but very different levels of crime as well. They found that the zone immediately surrounding the downtown area (i.e., the central business district) was populated chiefly by recent immigrants to the United States who needed the close access to employment available downtown and the cheap housing prices found in the deteriorating housing stock that had once served the earliest inhabitants of Chicago. In addition to the poor quality of the housing in those neighborhoods, however, the researchers also observed that this zone had the highest rates of crime in all of Chicago. Subsequently, Park and colleagues named this zone the *transitional zone* because individuals would typically move out of the zone as soon as they had the financial means to do so in order to escape the crime problems, only to be quickly replaced by an even newer cohort of immigrants who were also in need of access to downtown employment and cheap housing.[15]

---

[15] Individuals escaping the transitional zone typically moved to one of the three outer zones of Chicago identified by Park and colleagues – what they called the working class zone, the residential zone, and the suburban zone (listed from the nearest to the central business district to the furthest). Because these zones were not essential to Shaw and McKay's development of their theory of social disorganization, they are not discussed in any more detail here.

While most criminologists of the time believed that criminal behavior could be explained using characteristics of individuals, Park and colleagues' finding that the transitional zone consistently had the highest rates of crime in all of Chicago, regardless of who was living there at the time, paved the way for what was then a new way of thinking about crime. This new avenue for explaining criminal behavior was led by their colleagues, Clifford Shaw and Henry McKay. Based on Park and colleagues' finding, Shaw and McKay argued that, contrary to popular belief, it was not the people who lived in the transitional zone who caused rates of crime to be surprisingly high, rather it was the place in which they lived that gave rise to those high crime rates. In other words, Shaw and McKay believed that it was *places*, and not *people*, that were the key to explaining rates of crime.

Shaw and McKay's Theory of Social Disorganization

Using Park and colleagues' (1925) research as a foundation for their own work, Shaw and McKay's theory of social disorganization was a direct result of their attempts to explain the spatial variation in crime rates across the city of Chicago. This research ultimately led to their seminal work, *Juvenile Delinquency in Urban Areas* (1942), in which they first proposed linking neighborhood context to neighborhood juvenile arrest rates.[16] Although their original theory has received numerous additions and modifications, the fundamental argument remains the same - variation in neighborhood context influences the levels of crime, above and beyond the influences of the individual-level compositional factors related to the residents who live in them. Specifically, they argued that the negative effects of certain neighborhood structural characteristics would give rise to neighborhood residents being less likely and less able to come together, define, and ultimately achieve common goals, including the prevention of crime.

---

[16] While Shaw and McKay (1942) were primarily interested in explaining rates of juvenile delinquency and arrest rather than criminal behavior in general, their theory is commonly applied to the explanation of other forms of deviance and crime as well. Thus, for the purposes of this research, Shaw and McKay's original theory is considered to be an explanation for all types of crime, rather than juvenile delinquency only.

Furthermore, they argued that that the negative effects of those structural characteristics would lead to an increase in criminal values among neighborhood residents over time. Ultimately, it was the neighborhood's inability to collectively define and achieve common goals, as well as the increase in criminal values throughout the neighborhood that Shaw and McKay termed *social disorganization.*

The three neighborhood structural characteristics that Shaw and McKay believed would lead to neighborhood social disorganization were poverty, racial and/or ethnic heterogeneity, and residential instability, which collectively measure what will be referred to in this book as n*eighborhood structural disadvantage.*[17] Shaw and McKay found that Chicago's transitional zone consistently had not only the highest rates of crime, but it also had the highest rates of neighborhood structural disadvantage. As a result of this observation, Shaw and McKay argued that variation in a neighborhood's level of structural disadvantage would predict its level of neighborhood social organization (or the lack thereof), which would, in turn, predict its rates of crime.

To explain it more plainly, Shaw and McKay argued that because structurally disadvantaged neighborhoods were composed of many poor individuals (i.e., high levels of poverty), who were more likely to be of a variety of different cultural backgrounds (i.e., high levels of racial/ethnic heterogeneity), they would be unwilling, or unable, to get to know each other and agree on any common set of values and goals for the neighborhood as a whole. Then, exacerbating this problem, as many of the immigrants that populated the transitional zone assimilated into American culture and found better paying jobs, they would move away from the inner city and the transitional zone only to be replaced by new (poor racial/ethnic minority) families. The constant in- and out-flow of new residents (i.e., high levels of residential instability)

---

[17] Although Shaw and McKay do not coin a collective term for the three structural precursors of neighborhood social disorganization that they identified – poverty, racial/ethnic heterogeneity, and residential instability – for the remainder of this book, when *neighborhood structural disadvantage* is mentioned, it refers to the combined influence of all three of those neighborhood structural characteristics.

further complicating the remaining residents' ability to come together, get know each other, and form a common set of goals and values. Then, as this process repeated itself over the years, Shaw and McKay argued that it would quickly become nearly impossible for residents of those structurally disadvantaged neighborhoods to collectively define a set of rules regulating which behaviors were acceptable or unacceptable in their neighborhood. Consequently, the researchers expected that structurally disadvantaged neighborhoods would become more vulnerable to deviant and criminal activities since rules of behavior that did not exist could not be enforced. Unfortunately, Shaw and McKay would never explicitly give neighborhood residents' inability to regulate the behavior of individuals a specific name. Fortunately, however, later researchers would come to call the phenomena a *lack of informal social control* (e.g., Kornhauser 1978; Morenoff et al. 1997; Sampson et al. 1997; Sampson et al. 1999).

The lack of informal social control in structurally disadvantage neighborhoods was only one half of what Shaw and McKay meant when they said social disorganization, though. In order to help explain why neighborhoods within the transitional zone continued to consistently have high rates of crime over long periods of time, Shaw and McKay posited that neighborhood structural disadvantage not only reduced informal social control within a neighborhood, but that it also increased the deviant and criminal values among its residents. They contended that once high rates of crime had entered a neighborhood and become a regular occurrence, some residents would become accustomed to, and perhaps even tolerant of, a certain amount of criminal activity. Eventually, they believed that a subculture which actually embraced deviant and criminal values would form because no other residents of structurally disadvantaged neighborhoods would be willing to challenge those alternative values since there was no set of common values with which to begin. Effectively then, Shaw and McKay believed that deviant and criminal values might not only exist in disadvantaged neighborhoods, they could actually thrive and be transmitted from one generation of residents to another.[18] Thus, for

---

[18] While important in the original theory, Shaw and McKay's arguments regarding the transmission of deviant and criminal values have worked their way out of most contemporary research examining neighborhood social

Shaw and McKay, neighborhood social disorganization represented not only the inability of neighborhood residents to informally control deviant or criminal behavior, but also an increase in deviant and criminal values over time.

Unfortunately, while Shaw and McKay were able to observe a relationship between neighborhood structural disadvantage and juvenile arrest rates in Chicago, they never specifically sought to identify or empirically test any measures of neighborhood social disorganization. That is, even though they theorized about how social disorganization might mediate the relationship between neighborhood structural disadvantage and rates of crime, they never proposed how neighborhood informal social control efforts or deviant and criminal values might be operationalized. Subsequently, Shaw and McKay were only able to empirically link neighborhood structural disadvantage to increased rates of juvenile delinquency and arrests (but not their actual concept of neighborhood social disorganization). Then, perhaps as a result of this omission, their theory fell out of favor among criminologists for several decades until the work of some new researchers once again sparked interest in the field of neighborhoods and crime.

The Informal Social Control Reformulation

More than three decades after Shaw and McKay unveiled their original theory of social disorganization, Kornhauser (1978) published her dissertation research on what she generally described as "the social sources of delinquency." In her dissertation, she both lauded and critiqued Shaw and McKay's original theory. While she agreed with their conclusion that places were important factors for explaining crime, she was also one of the first people to criticize Shaw and McKay for not clearly enough explicating the mechanisms through which they expected neighborhood structural disadvantage to lead to increased

---

disorganization. For the widely-accepted argument regarding why the concept of deviant and criminal values should have never been included in their original theory, see the review of Kornhauser's (1978) contributions to the social disorganization tradition below.

rates of crime (i.e., neighborhood social disorganization). And, it was through this criticism of Shaw and McKay's theory that Kornhauser ultimately made two of the most important contributions to the greater social disorganization tradition.

Kornhauser's first major contribution to the social disorganization tradition was her insistence that the Shaw and McKay's concept of *informal social control* should receive a greater emphasis. She argued that criminologists needed to more seriously consider how neighborhood residents' willingness to intervene on behalf of their neighborhood and regulate behaviors, without the help of formal sources of control (i.e., the police), might influence neighborhood rates of crime. Moreover, while her definition of informal social control was very similar to what Shaw and McKay (1942) described in their work (but never officially named), she focused less on residents sharing common goals and values, and argued that more attention should be paid to residents' collective willingness to *act* when their neighborhood was threatened. In other words, Kornhauser argued that neighborhood structural disadvantage would make residents less willing to place themselves in harm's way for the benefit of their neighbors, and consequently, the neighborhood would have no one to step forward and put a stop to any deviant or criminal behaviors. Only then, when no one was willing to act, did she believe that a neighborhood would become vulnerable to being taken over by criminal activity. Thus, Kornhauser's first major contributions to the social disorganization tradition was the increased emphasis that she placed on residents' ability to informally regulate behaviors in their neighborhood (i.e., neighborhood informal social control).

Kornhauser's second major contribution to the social disorganization tradition might actually be considered a case of addition by subtraction. She contended that Shaw and McKay's (1942) subcultural argument regarding the inter-generational transmission of criminal values contradicted their other arguments regarding how neighborhood structural disadvantage would lead to increased rates of crime. She argued that, because Shaw and McKay expected that the residents of structurally disadvantaged neighborhoods were unable to come together and form and enforce common values that would condemn deviant behaviors and crime, they should just as well be unable to come together and form and enforce common values that would *promote deviant behaviors and crime.* Simply put, she questioned why Shaw and McKay believed that neighborhood residents could come to an agreement that deviant and criminal behaviors should be acceptable, when they had argued in the some piece that those same people could not come together to agree on anything else.

In addition to this critique of the subcultural component of Shaw and McKay's original theory of social disorganization, Kornhauser also criticized the researchers for trying to explain the consistently high rates of crime in structurally disadvantage neighborhoods through the inter-generational transmission of criminal values. She argued that because structurally disadvantaged neighborhoods had high levels of residential instability, each successive wave of immigrants (or other new groups) who moved into those neighborhoods should continue to experience social disorganization and consequently have high rates of crime. Then, if residential instability could explain high rates of crime over time, she believed that using the transmission of culture as an explanation for the same phenomenon was not only redundant, but unnecessary. Based on this logic, Kornhauser argued that if neighborhood residential instability could explain high levels of social disorganization and crime over time, then there was never really any need to introduce the concept of inter-generationally transmitted criminal values (i.e., criminal subcultures) and strongly recommended that it should therefore be purged from the tradition (although some argue that it should be brought back – e.g., Anderson 1999; Warner 2003).

Kornhauser's two major contributions to the evolution of the social disorganization tradition were therefore 1) that a stronger emphasis be placed on the role neighborhood informal social control efforts, and 2) that the subcultural element of Shaw and McKay's original theory be cut out. Despite what contemporary social disorganization theorists now recognize as being invaluable contributions, however, at the time in which Kornhauser's dissertation was published, the social disorganization tradition remained relatively unpopular. It was not until two new social-disorganization-based explanations of neighborhood crime rates emerged in the early 1990s that the tradition finally experienced a popular revival.

The Systemic Model

Almost a decade after Kornhauser's contribution to the social disorganization tradition, several researchers separately began arguing for even more revisions to Shaw and McKay's original theory. Although Granovetter (1973) and Kasarda and Janowitz (1974) are credited with first acknowledging the importance of social ties and social networks, it was a number of later researchers who are credited with the creation of *the systemic model* of social disorganization (Bursik and Grasmick 1993; Hunter 1985; Sampson and Groves 1989). These researchers contended that Shaw and McKay (1942) and Kornhauser (1978) missed an important mediating factor in their explanations of the relationship between neighborhood structural disadvantage and rates of crime. They argued that the existence of strong and frequent social ties amongst neighborhood residents were essential if one expected those residents to willingly step in and intervene on behalf of their neighborhood to regulate unacceptable behaviors (i.e., exercise informal social control). If those ties did not exist, they continued, then residents would be unwilling to put themselves in harm's way for the benefit of their neighbors or their neighborhood. As a result, the researchers expected levels of informal of social control to be very low in neighborhoods where the social ties among residents were few or very weak, ultimately resulting in the neighborhood becoming more vulnerable to criminal activity.

The notion of neighborhood social ties described above, which is at the heart of the neighborhood systemic model, draws heavily from the work of Kasarda and Janowitz (1974).[19] These researchers argued

---

[19] The concept of social ties can also be traced back to the work of Granovetter (1973). Unlike Kasarda and Janowitz (1974), Granovetter argued for the strength of *weak* ties. He contended that weak ties to other individuals in a social network were sufficient to effectively transmit information and be beneficial to members of the network. While later researchers acknowledged the importance of weak neighborhood social ties (see review below), the original founders of the neighborhood systemic model perspective believed that *strong ties* and *large social networks* were the key to explaining high levels of informal social control and the consequently lower levels of neighborhood crime.

that social ties and social networks were important aspects of neighborhoods that strongly influenced how residents interacted with each other. If ties were weak, and networks were small, they argued, then residents would be more likely to keep to themselves and less likely to become involved in the affairs of their neighbors. If ties were strong and networks were extensive, on the other hand, then Kasarda and Janowitz expected that residents would be more likely to socialize and become friends with their neighbors and ultimately become more involved in the business of the neighborhood as a whole.

Based on the above ideas, proponents of the systemic model (Bursik and Grasmick 1993; Hunter 1985; Sampson and Groves 1989), argued that neighborhood structural disadvantage reduced residents' ability to make ties to one another or to their neighborhood, which would in turn make them less willing to step in on behalf of those neighbors or their neighborhood to regulate deviant or criminal behavior, eventually resulting in increased criminal activity. Thus, according to systemic model theorists, both Shaw and McKay and Kornhauser missed an important mediating mechanism – neighborhood social ties – that could help explain why structurally disadvantaged neighborhoods had lower levels of informal social control and, ultimately, higher crime rates.

In addition to providing the social disorganization tradition with another mechanism for explaining how and why neighborhood structural disadvantage might be related to neighborhood levels of crime, systemic model researchers were also the first to empirically measure and test the viability of their arguments. Regrettably, as reviewed in more detail below, even though the systemic model has received much scholarly attention, the findings in regards to its viability as an explanation of neighborhood crime rates have been largely inconsistent. Nonetheless, proponents of the systemic model made important contributions to the social disorganization tradition not only by identifying another potential mechanism for consideration, but also by being the first researchers to empirically assess the direct, indirect, and mediating effects of various neighborhood contextual factors (including neighborhood structural disadvantage and social ties) on neighborhood rates of crime.

The Emergence of a Collective Efficacy Framework

The most recent modification to the social disorganization tradition comes in the form of another mediating mechanism of the relationship between neighborhood structural disadvantage and neighborhood crime rates – *collective efficacy*. The concept of collective efficacy is attributed to Sampson and a number of his colleagues (Morenoff et al. 2001; Sampson et al. 1999; Sampson et al. 1997). Despite the recent theoretical and empirical development of the systemic model, Sampson and colleagues argued that social ties among neighborhood residents were not as important for linking neighborhood structural disadvantage to neighborhood rates of crime as previous researchers had suggested (Bursik and Grasmick 1993; Hunter 1985; Sampson and Groves 1989).

Sampson and colleagues also believed that Kornhauser's (1978) exclusive focus on neighborhood informal social control was too narrow, however. As a result, they believed that only an agreement on common goals and values, and more importantly, a mutual trust amongst neighbors that every resident of the neighborhood would be willing to intervene and exercise informal social control efforts would be sufficient to prevent social disorganization and ultimately crime. Moreover, they believed that residents did not need to have frequent or strong social ties with their neighbors, as long as they trusted them to engage in informal social control efforts when necessary. Sampson and colleagues therefore defined neighborhood collective efficacy as the combination of two concepts – informal social control (i.e., the willingness to intervene on behalf of the neighborhood) *and* social cohesion (i.e., the sharing of common beliefs, values, and a mutual trust among residents).[20]

Using these concepts, Sampson and colleagues hypothesized that high levels of neighborhood structural disadvantage would impair residents' ability to get together, define common goals and values, and

---

[20] Although social cohesion may appear to be very similar in nature to the systemic model's notion of social ties, the focus here is more on the relationship among *all* neighborhood residents, rather than a few strong ties among friends and family members. In essence, Sampson and colleagues' concept of social cohesion is consistent with the notion of weak ties described in detail by Bellair (1997) (see also, Granovetter 1973).

most importantly, trust each other. They then argued that, even if residents had strong social networks within their neighborhood, if they could not trust the individuals within those networks to engage in informal social control, they would be unwilling to make any effort themselves. As a result of this lack of mutual trust, Sampson and colleagues believed that informal social control efforts in the neighborhood would be weakened, leaving the residents vulnerable to deviant and criminal activities, even in the presence of strong social ties.

It should be noted that, unlike the previous modifications and reformulations of Shaw and McKay's original theory discussed previously, Sampson and colleagues' concept of neighborhood collective efficacy actually serves as a measure of neighborhood social *organization*. In other words, whereas Kornhauser and the proponents of the systemic model generally defined neighborhood social disorganization as the presence of *low* levels of informal social control, Sampson and colleagues combined *high* levels of informal social control with their concept of social cohesion so that they were measuring the inverse of social *dis*organization. Rather than using neighborhood social disorganization to predict high rates of crime then, Sampson and colleagues effectively used neighborhood collective efficacy to predict lower neighborhood crime rates. Despite this departure from earlier conceptualizations of neighborhood social disorganization, the concept of collective efficacy is nonetheless consistent with the larger social disorganization tradition since its proponents are still trying to explain why neighborhood structural disadvantage might be related to neighborhood rates of crime.

Like systemic model researchers, Sampson and colleagues also contributed to the theoretical development of the social disorganization tradition by conducting empirical tests of the mechanisms that they proposed. Unlike tests of the systemic model, however, research on neighborhood collective efficacy has been largely supportive of the framework. Perhaps not surprisingly then, Sampson and colleagues' contributions to the development of the social disorganization tradition include not only the conceptualization and empirical assessment of their collective efficacy concept, but also the revival of scholarly and popular interest in the study of neighborhoods and crime.

Empirical Tests of the Social Disorganization Tradition

Since Shaw and McKay first proposed their original theory of social disorganization, numerous studies have empirically analyzed many of the concepts and mechanisms associated with the tradition, including neighborhood structural disadvantage, informal social control, the systemic model (i.e., social ties), and collective efficacy (i.e., informal social control *and* neighborhood social cohesion). Beginning with the individual effects of neighborhood structural disadvantage's component measures (poverty, racial/ethnic heterogeneity, and residential stability), researchers have consistently found very strong support for nearly all of the social disorganization concepts reviewed above in regards to their capacity to explain neighborhood rates of crime.

Although astute social disorganization tradition researchers recognize that Shaw and McKay never actually hypothesized that neighborhood structural disadvantage was directly related to neighborhood crimes (as reviewed above, they expected the effect to be mediated by a loss of informal social control and an increase in criminal values), nearly all of the empirical research on the subject has nonetheless attempted to discern both the direct and indirect effects of neighborhood structural disadvantage on rates of crime. And, almost without exception, such research has observed a positive and significant relationship between the component measures of neighborhood structural disadvantage and neighborhood crime rates. More simply put, researchers have found that as neighborhood levels of poverty, racial/ethnic heterogeneity, and residential instability[21] increase, so do levels of crime and delinquency (e.g., Bursik and Grasmick 1993; Krivo and Peterson 1996; Morenoff et al. 1997; Peterson, Krivo, and Harris 2000; Sampson and Groves 1989; Sampson

---

[21] While the role of neighborhood structural disadvantage in general is one of the most well-established in all of the neighborhoods and crime literature, the independent effect of residential instability has been observed to be the weakest (Sampson et al. 2002). Nonetheless, with a large body of supporting literature, all three measures of neighborhood structural disadvantage should be included in any study of neighborhood context, and are therefore also included in this analysis of police use of excessive force.

et al. 1997; Sampson et al. 1999; Sampson et al. 2001; Shaw and McKay 1942; Silver 2000; Warner and Rountree 1997; Veysey and Messner 1999; for a comprehensive review see Sampson, Morenoff, and Gannon-Rowley 2002).

Research examining the specific influence of neighborhood informal social control efforts on crime rates has been largely supportive as well. As Kornhauser (1978) first hypothesized, the empirical research has shown that when residents are willing to intervene on behalf of their neighborhood to prevent deviant and criminal behaviors, crime rates tend to be low (Hunter 1985; Bursik 1999; Kornhauser 1978; Velez 2001; Veysey and Messner 1999). Moreover, much of the research that has included measures of neighborhood informal control as a part of Sampson and colleagues' collective efficacy has also found it to be negatively and significantly related to rates of crime (see detailed review below).[22] Neighborhood informal social control therefore appears to be an important contextual factor for predicting levels of crime as well.

While the importance of neighborhood structural disadvantage and informal social control have been widely supported and recognized in the neighborhoods and crime literature, researchers have not come to the same level of consensus regarding the importance of social ties in a neighborhood. In the first empirical test of the neighborhood systemic model, Sampson and Groves (1989) examined how neighborhood structural disadvantage affected neighborhood residents' participation in both formal (e.g., neighborhood or condominium associations) and informal or voluntary (e.g., neighborhood watch programs) organizations, the breadth of neighborhood friendship networks, and the extent to which unsupervised teenage peer groups existed. They found that in neighborhoods where participation in formal organizations was low and where neighborhood friendship networks were weak, unsupervised teenage peer groups strongly and significantly

---

[22] As one of the primary goals of this research is to test Sampson and colleagues' concept of collective efficacy as an explanation for police officers' use of excessive force, rather than examining the independent effect of neighborhoods informal social control efforts, it is analyzed only as a component of the collective efficacy measure. For more details on how the concept of informal social control is utilized within this research, see Chapter 5.

predicted higher rates of crime, thereby providing some initial support for their systemic model of social disorganization.

Since Sampson and Groves' original research testing their systemic model, a number of researchers have attempted to replicate their findings, to varying degrees of success (e.g., Lowencamp, Cullen, and Pratt 2003; Sun, Triplett, and Gainey 2004; Veysey and Messner 1999). Other researchers, however, have argued that in many neighborhoods with low rates of crime, residents may not always have strong or frequent social ties or networks with the other members of their neighborhood, and many residents may not even have frequent interactions with any of their neighbors (e.g., Patillo-McCoy 1999; Sampson et al. 1997; Wilson 1996). These researchers suggested that the residents of many low-crime neighborhoods are likely to have their strongest social ties and social networks with individuals *outside* of their neighborhood (i.e., with family, school, or work friends that live in other areas), subsequently leaving few strong or frequent ties to their actual neighbors. And, while much of the research just mentioned was theoretical or based on qualitative evidence with limited generalizability, other recent empirical analyses of large-scale survey data has not only supported such suppositions, but some has even indicated that strong neighborhood social ties may actually *increase* neighborhood rates of crime.

First, drawing on Granovetter's (1973) piece, "The Strength of Weak Ties," Bellair (1997) found that infrequent social contact and weak social ties predicted lower levels of crime just as well, if not better, than frequent social contact and strong ties (although the greatest reductions in crime occurred in the presence of both weak *and* strong social ties). Moreover, he observed that neighborhood informal social control efforts were just as likely to occur in neighborhoods that had infrequent social contact and weak social ties amongst residents as they were to occur in neighborhoods with frequent contact and strong ties. Subsequently, Bellair concluded that weak social ties amongst neighbors (i.e., those ties among non-family, non-friend neighbors) might actually be more important predictors of informal social control efforts, and ultimately lower rates of crime, than stronger neighborhood social ties.

In addition to Bellair's findings, other recent empirical evidence has suggested that strong neighborhood social ties may actually impede informal social control efforts, thereby resulting in *increases*, rather than decreases, in neighborhood levels of crime. For example, in their research examining the influence of both neighborhood social ties and collective efficacy, Browning, Feinberg, and Dietz (2004) observed that collective efficacy was the better predictor of low neighborhood crime rates, and that strong neighborhood social ties were actually related to higher neighborhood crime rates. In light of these findings, Browning and colleagues concluded that having many strong social ties within a neighborhood might actually shield criminals from both informal and formal social control efforts. Specifically, they posited that if criminals had strong familial or friendship ties to other residents within their neighborhood, then those residents might protect them from social control efforts (formal or informal), and in doing so, allow those individuals to continue offending, and ultimately driving up neighborhood crime rates.

Finally, Sampson and colleagues (1997) both theorized and found empirical evidence challenging the importance of neighborhood social ties. To briefly reiterate their position, Sampson and colleagues firmly believed that neighborhood residents did not need to have strong or frequent social ties, as long as they shared a mutual trust that their neighbors were willing to exercise informal social control efforts when necessary. And, just as they expected, Sampson and his various colleagues found strong empirical support for their hypothesis that high levels of collective efficacy within a neighborhood would reduce those neighborhoods' crime rates (Morenoff et al. 1997; Sampson et al. 1997; Sampson et al. 1999; Sampson et al. 2001; Sampson et al. 2002), even in the absence of large social networks or strong social ties amongst neighbors. However, one might be skeptical of Sampson and colleagues' research which had all supported the collective efficacy framework since they were the same researchers who developed it in the first place. Auspiciously, other neighborhoods and crime researchers have also consistently found support for the collective efficacy framework, though, lending both credence and generalizability to Sampson and colleagues' own research.

A number of other social disorganization researchers have recently conducted empirical tests of the collective efficacy framework and each has observed a strong, negative, and significant relationship between the concept and a variety of aggregate-level measures of crime and deviance (Browning 2002; Browning et al. 2004; Cancino 2005; Reisig and Cancino 2004; Triplett et al. 2003). Thus, while a not unsubstantial body of research has called into question the relative importance of neighborhood social ties,[23] the ameliorative role of collective efficacy on neighborhood rates of crime appears to be above reproach. Neighborhood collective efficacy has therefore been, and continues to be today, one of the most prominent modifications of the social disorganization tradition.

---

[23] Based on the empirical evidence reviewed here, neighborhood social ties appear to be less influential than some researchers had originally envisioned. Nonetheless, in order to fully test the viability of the social disorganization tradition as a theoretical framework for explaining police officers' use of excessive force, measures of both neighborhood social ties (i.e., the systemic model) *and* collective efficacy (measured as informal social control and neighborhood social cohesion) are included in this research.

CHAPTER 4

Why Neighborhood Context May Influence Police Use of Force

Researchers have long studied both the causes of police use of force and the importance of neighborhood context in the explanation of crime, but in the history of both disciplines, rarely have the subjects theoretically or empirically dovetailed. To date, only a handful of inspired researchers have attempted to bring together any concepts or methodologies from the policing and neighborhoods and crime fields to study police use of force within the context of socially disorganized neighborhoods. Moreover, since the reemergence of the social disorganization tradition in the 1980s and 1990s, even the few studies that have actually utilized neighborhood-level contextual measures to predict police officers' use of force, none have specifically used a theoretical framework based on the social disorganization tradition as a whole to explain why officers might use excessive force in disorganized areas. Instead, those few studies that have empirically tested concepts from the tradition have generally conducted variable-driven research that fails to offer any theoretical explanations for their results. Furthermore, even though policing researchers have begun to embrace some of the more advanced multi-level modeling techniques commonly utilized by neighborhoods and crime researchers, none have done so to the full extent of the techniques' capabilities.

Neighborhood Context and Police Use of Force

Only four empirical studies have attempted to examine the relationship between aggregate-level contextual factors and police officers' use of force (Kane 2002; Lawton 2007; Lersch, Bazley, Mieczkowski, and Childs 2008; Terrill and Reisig 2003). Unfortunately, while each of these studies has utilized concepts from the social disorganization tradition, none has actually developed a theoretical framework as a foundation for explaining *why* those concepts should be related to police use of force behavior. Moreover, only one has actually studied neighborhoods, in comparison to alternative levels of aggregation

(Terrill and Reisig 2003). Nonetheless, such research provides clues as to which aggregate-level contextual factors might be related to police officers' use of force. Additionally, three of the four (with the exception of Lersch et al. 2008) studies utilized multi-level modeling techniques, and help to demonstrate how research on policing can benefit from a more widespread incorporation of such advanced techniques. Despite such important contributions, however, each of the studies is flawed in some way that makes drawing conclusions about the viability of a social disorganization explanation of police use of force difficult, if not impossible.

In the most recent study to consider neighborhood contextual effects, Lersch and colleagues (2008) empirically tested whether various measures of structural disadvantage could be linked to police officers' use of force in one unidentified city in the Southeastern US. Data for their dependent measure came from official use-of-force report forms (that must be completed any time an officer uses force against a civilian), as reported by the local municipal department's officers. In order to measure neighborhood structural disadvantage, they used census block groups as proxies for neighborhoods and measured the percentage of each tract that was non-white, headed by females with children, and that were either rentals, or vacant.[24] They also controlled for tract-level crime rates (violent and property crimes per 1,000 residents) and the number of active resistance incidents (officer reports of individuals who attempted to physically defeat control efforts or injure officers).

Lersch and colleagues then conducted negative binomial regression analyses (they are the only study of neighborhood context

---

[24] Although the Lersch and colleagues' (2008) four measures of structural disadvantage are slightly different than those commonly utilized by social disorganization researchers to assess neighborhood levels of poverty, racial/ethnic heterogeneity, and residential instability (see the measures used for this research discussed in Chapter 5), their measures are generally considered to still be good indicators of the same broad concept that Shaw and McKay (1942) originally envisioned and have been used (primarily as supplements to the standard measures) by other researchers studying neighborhoods and crime (for a review, see Sampson et al. 2002).

and police use of force not to utilize multi-level modeling techniques) and found that only the number of active resistance incidents and percentage non-white significantly predicted increases in police officers use of force, net of their other controls (although both crime rate measures and percent female-headed households significantly predicted police use of force when the number of active resistance incidents were not included in their models). Subsequently, even though their research is a step in the right direction, their findings provide only partial support for the capacity of social disorganization concepts to explain police use of force.

The study conducted by Lersch and colleagues suffers from a number of noteworthy flaws, however, that should lead shrewd researchers to take their findings with that proverbial grain of salt. First, Lersch and colleagues do not actually use real neighborhoods as their unit of analysis. Census tracts and census tract block-groups are notoriously imprecise estimations of true neighborhoods (for a detailed discussion, see Chapter 5). Second, the researchers did not conduct a multi-level analysis that would have allowed them to control for individual-level "neighborhood" compositional effects (for a detailed review, once again see Chapter 5). Finally, although they included measures of structural disadvantage, Lersch and colleagues did not specifically utilize the social disorganization tradition to frame their research, rather they only borrowed one of its concepts. Unfortunately, however, because many concepts from the social disorganization tradition might also be used as measures of the social threat theoretical framework (i.e., researchers could make a pretty compelling argument that percentage non-white, female-headed households, and rental units could all be used to measure the minority populations that pose a threat to the existing social hierarchy), without expressly identifying and laying out their arguments for how they test a specific theoretical framework, their research cannot, and should not, be considered an actual test of the social disorganization tradition.

In a second study empirically linking neighborhood contextual factors and police use of force, Lawton (2007) tested how a variety of individual- and contextual-factors influenced the amount of (legitimate) force police officers used on civilians. Using data from the Philadelphia Police Department in 2002, Lawton conducted a multi-level analysis of individual police-civilian encounters with a number of police district-level controls for violent crime rates and racial heterogeneity (percentage of each police district that was African American). Although Lawton never intended for his police districts to approximate actual neighborhoods, his findings do shed some light on how the effect of aggregate-level predictors on police use of force can vary across geographic space.

Lawton found that district-level violent crime rates were positively related to police officers' use of higher levels of non-lethal force ($p < 0.15$), but only when individual-level factors related to the police-civilian encounter (e.g., officer and civilian race and gender, and civilian behavior during the encounter) were not included in his model. Additionally, he found that racial heterogeneity was negatively related to police use of force, this time net of individual-level encounter controls ($p < 0.15$). As a consequent of the relaxed significance levels that Lawton reported, however, it is once again difficult to draw any firm conclusions from his work.

Nevertheless, like Lersch and colleagues (2008), Lawton's research provides some additional, if not provisional, evidence that racial heterogeneity may be related to police use of force behavior at the aggregate-level. Unfortunately once again, though, because Lawton tested only one concept from the social disorganization tradition, and because he did not specifically use the tradition to frame his research, it is difficult to conclude that his research is truly supportive a social disorganization effect on police use of force, rather than a social threat one. Moreover, because he measured racial heterogeneity at the district-level (rather than the neighborhood-level), it is unlikely that he accurately captured the contextual effect of neighborhoods on police behavior. Despite these reservations in regards to his findings, however, Lawton's study takes a step in the right direction by being one of only two extant studies that test both individual- and aggregate-level predictors of police use of force simultaneously using multi-level modeling techniques.[25]

Kane (2002) takes another step towards legitimizing a potential relationship between neighborhood social disorganization and police

---

[25] See the review of Terrill and Reisig (2003) below.

officers' use of force. Using two concepts from the social disorganization tradition – concentrated disadvantage and residential instability – Kane attempted to predict variation in police officer misconduct (including, but not specific to, police officers' use of excessive force). He created his concentrated disadvantage and residential mobility variables using U.S. census data in the same fashion as originally constructed by Sampson and colleagues' (1997) measures (see Sampson et al. 1997 for a discussion). He then utilized data from official police records for 75 New York City police precincts, within 20 larger police divisions, between 1975 and 1996 to conduct a multi-level analysis of police misconduct over time. The results of his analyses revealed that both disadvantage and mobility were positively and significantly related to police misconduct at both the precinct- and division-level.

The results of Kane's study provide compelling evidence that aggregate-level concepts related to the social disorganization tradition may truly be related to police officers use of force. Unfortunately, as with both Lersch and colleagues (2008) and Lawton's (2007) studies, Kane's study is simply not a rigorous enough test of the relationship between neighborhood social disorganization and police use of force for a number of reasons. First, although his dependent variable measured police use of excessive force (which is the primary variable of interest for this research), it was actually a scale measure of a number of types of police misconduct, including corruption, administrative policy violations, and drug test failures. Because he did not disaggregate his dependent variable by type of misconduct, it is impossible to determine how well his explanatory variables (including the two concepts from the social disorganization tradition) actually predicted variation in police officers' use of excessive force in particular. Second, like those two other studies, Kane did not actually examine neighborhood-level effects. Instead, he analyzed precinct- and division-level effects and made no effort to discuss how those aggregations might compare to neighborhoods. Thus, even though he found significant effects for concentrated disadvantage and residential mobility (which better measure neighborhood social disorganization than either of the two previously reviewed studies reviewed), his levels of aggregation are a concern. Third, Kane's multi-level analysis did not examine any individual-level predictors of police misconduct.

Although he conducted a multi-level analysis, he used two aggregate levels, precincts and divisions, and did not control for any of the individual-level factors that may also influence police misconduct. Finally, while he utilized concepts from the social disorganization tradition, he made no attempt to explain why those concepts should be related to police misconduct. As a consequence, Kane's study, like the ones reviewed above, provides tentative, but by no means definitive, evidence that aggregate-level contextual measures might be related to police use of excessive force.

Finally, in the only piece to specifically claim to examine neighborhood contextual effects, Terrill and Reisig (2003) used observational data from the Project on Policing Neighborhoods (POPN) study to examine whether neighborhood concentrated disadvantage influenced the level of force police officers used on crime suspects, net of neighborhood levels of crime and a host of individual-level controls related to police-suspect encounters. The results of their multi-level analysis revealed that police officers were more likely to use higher levels of force on individuals who they encountered in disadvantaged neighborhoods (concentrated disadvantage was measured following the lead of Sampson et al. [1997] as well) as compared to individuals who they encountered in better neighborhoods (i.e., those with lower levels of disadvantage). For the very first time then, Terrill and Reisig were able to specifically demonstrate that *neighborhood* context could in fact predict police officers' use of force.

Unfortunately, just as with the cases of each of the other studies reviewed thus far, there are limitations of Terrill and Reisig's study that must be taken into consideration before any broader conclusions can be drawn. First, the researchers tested only one concept from the social disorganization tradition (concentrated disadvantage), although they do measure it in the same way, and at the same level of aggregation, as other social disorganization researchers commonly do (unlike the three previous studies). And, while they observed a statistically significant relationship ($p < 0.05$), including only one measure of disorganization should still not be considered a rigorous enough test of the relationship between neighborhood social disorganization and police use of force. Second, Terrill and Reisig examined the influence of concentrated disadvantage on only the legitimate use of force by the police.

Subsequently, it is still unclear whether or not neighborhood context can specifically predict police officers' use of *excessive* force. Finally, just as the three studies reviewed above failed to do, Terrill and Reisig once again fail to offer any theoretical explanations for why neighborhood context should influence police officers' use of force behaviors. Consequently, even though their study provides the strongest evidence of a relationship between neighborhood context and police use of force thus far, it only begins to address the object of this research, which is to propose and empirically test a social disorganization theory of police use of *excessive* force.

To briefly review, the four primary criticisms of all four studies discussed above were 1) they did actually use the social disorganization tradition as a framework to explain how or the related concepts should have been related to police use of force, 2) they examined only measures of structural disadvantage (but never all three at the same time) and did not consider the effects of any other important social disorganization concepts (i.e., neighborhood social ties and collective efficacy), 3) they did not accurately estimate actual neighborhoods in three of the four studies (with the exception being Terrill and Reisig [2003]), and finally, 4) they failed to use multi-level modeling techniques to their fullest extent which might have allowed them to better distinguish individual-level compositional factors from neighborhood contextual factors.[26] Thus, even though the four studies reviewed above provide some tentative evidence which suggests that aggregate-level contextual factors might viably be used to predict police officers' use of force, the primary objective of this book is to address each of the above criticisms and for the first time reliably demonstrate the viability of a social disorganization theory of police use of force.[27]

Linking Social Disorganization to Police Use of Force

As the four studies reviewed above perfectly demonstrate, perhaps the most essential condition for convincingly linking neighborhood social

---

[26] For a detailed discussion of this issue, see Chapter 5.

[27] Only the first criticism is addressed in this chapter (in the following section). The three other criticisms are addressed in Chapter 5.

disorganization to police officers' use of force is precisely formulating the theoretical mechanisms and/or processes that connect the phenomena. In particular, it is necessary to illustrate exactly how and why police officers working in disorganized neighborhoods might be more inclined to use force – especially excessive levels of force.

As reviewed in Chapter 3, the social disorganization tradition predicts that crime rates will be the highest in neighborhoods where structural disadvantage (poverty, racial/ethnic heterogeneity, and residential instability) leads to a decrease in neighborhood informal social control, social ties, and collective efficacy, rendering those neighborhoods more vulnerable to crime. Increased crime rates might not be the only negative consequence of disorganization, though. In the same way the social disorganization signals to criminals that they will be able to get away with criminal activities (because residents lack the social ties and/or collective efficacy to stop them), it may also signal to police officers that they will be able to get away with the use of excessive force. To exacerbate the issue, the higher crime rates typically found in those neighborhoods should send an even stronger signal to the officers working in those neighborhoods that the residents are incapable of controlling any type of deviant behavior, whether they are criminal acts committed by civilians or the use of excessive force by the police. In order to more fully flesh out the potential processes and mechanisms through which neighborhood social disorganization might lead to police use of excessive force, though, it is useful to discuss the subject in more detail.

The link between neighborhood social disorganization and crime rates is well-established (for a detailed review, see Sampson et al. 2002). In socially disorganized neighborhoods, residents come to rely on formal forms of social control (i.e., the police) more heavily since, by definition, they lack the collective capacity to handle the problems that arise in their neighborhoods on their own. In other words, where high levels of structural disadvantage lead to a loss of social ties and collective efficacy, neighborhood residents lack the means necessary to "police" themselves. Consequently, without these means, it is logical to assume that socially disorganized neighborhoods will have a greater dependence on *formal* forms of social control than neighborhoods that are able to "police" themselves. And, in fact, there has been empirical research which has shown that neighborhood social disorganization is positively and significantly related to calls for police services (Sherman, Gartin, and Buerger 1989; Warner and Pierce 1993).

The fact that socially disorganized neighborhoods come to rely more heavily on the police to resolve their crime problems has multiple implications. First, an increased dependence of neighborhood residents on formal police action may further impair residents' collective capacity to solve problems on their own. That is, if they continuously rely on outside sources of control, they may become dependent on them completely, such that neighborhood residents no longer even consider handling problems informally. Second, while the increased dependence on formal social controls may increase police officers' presence in the neighborhood, it might also send a message to criminals that the neighborhood is vulnerable to victimization any time the police are not present. Consequently, overall rates of crime may not decrease, as criminals simply shift their activities to times and locations when and where the police are not present. Finally, and of most importance for this research, social disorganization, and the lack of collective efficacy in particular, may also signal to police officers that their own deviant behavior, including the use of excessive force, will very likely go unreported and unpunished.

Given this last point, it might be reasonable to question whether police officers actually notice things such as neighborhood social disorganization. That is, will police officers realize not only that they are working in a high crime neighborhood, but also one that has no social ties and/or collective efficacy? And, if they do notice, would they pass such information on to their fellow officers to the extent that overall rates of police use of excessive force would substantially increase? Research has found that police officers do recognize the seriousness of crime problems in the neighborhoods in which they work, and that they do discuss such issues amongst their colleagues (McLaughlin, Johnson, Bowers, Birks, and Pease 2007; Ratcliffe and McCulagh 2001; Rengert 1995). And, even though there has not been any empirical research considering whether police officers discuss things such as neighborhood social disorganization, it seems reasonable that if police officers recognize and discuss the crime problems associated with certain neighborhoods, they should probably also recognized and discuss their use of force in those same neighborhoods, and in particular, how the neighborhood residents responded to it (or, alternatively, how they failed to respond to it).

Based on this reasoning, as police officers come to realize that residents of socially disorganized neighborhoods lack the capacity to informally deal with the crime problems facing their neighborhoods (i.e., without police assistance), they may also realize that those same residents are unable to organize to prevent, deter, and/or bring about punishment for police officers' use of excessive force. Subsequently, if even just one officer proceeded to share such information with his or her fellow officers working in the same neighborhood, an increase in the overall rate of police use of excessive might result. In the end, socially disorganized neighborhoods would then have just one more problem which they could not handle and nowhere else to turn for help, ultimately leaving the residents of those neighborhoods doubly-victimized – both by the criminals who offend in their neighborhoods and by the police officers who were supposed to protect them.

Before proposing the specific research questions and hypotheses that will be focus of this research, however, it is important to understand three points about the arguments presented above. First, research has shown that police officers' use of force, though rare, is more common when dealing with criminals (U.S. Department of Justice 2005). Subsequently, it should be expected that police officers will use more force in socially disorganized neighborhoods as compared to socially organized neighborhoods simply because they deal with more criminals in disorganized neighborhoods and it takes at least some force for officers to arrest those individuals (e.g., handcuffing criminal suspects).

The primary difference between socially organized and socially disorganized neighborhoods may then lie in whether or not the police officers use force on *non*-criminal residents as well. That is, if both criminals *and* non-criminal neighborhood residents of socially disorganized neighborhoods have force used upon them, those neighborhoods should experience relatively greater levels of police use of force than their socially organized counterparts. And, because any unjustified use of force on individuals who have not committed a crime must be considered "excessive," if the police use any force on non-criminal residents of disorganized neighborhoods, those neighborhoods should have greater problems with the police use of excessive force as a whole.[28]

Based on the discussion above, it can therefore be expected that, in addition to the "normal" levels of force police officers use against neighborhood criminals (i.e., the force necessary to effect arrests), the *additional* use of force on *non*-criminal residents should result in socially disorganized neighborhoods experiencing both an increased amount of police use of legitimate force *and* an increased amount of police use of excessive force compared to their socially organized counterparts. Then, on top of the illegitimate, and therefore excessive, use of force on non-criminal residents of socially disorganized neighborhoods, police officers may also be more likely to use more force than is necessary to arrest neighborhood criminals, which must also be considered excessive force. Consequently, in comparison to the residents of socially organized neighborhoods, both the criminal and non-criminal residents of socially disorganized neighborhoods may have much more problems with police officers' use of excessive force.

Second, it is in no way expected that *all* police officers working in socially disorganized neighborhoods will use excessive levels of force. In fact, it should be understood that the vast majority of police officers are *not* expected to use excessive force, even if they realized that they might be able to get away with it. Instead, the basic argument made here is that *some* police officers might realize that their use of force in disorganized neighborhoods was much less likely to gain widespread public attention or result in their formal punishment. Then, even if it was only a few "bad apples" who used more excessive force, the overall rate of police use of excessive force in those neighborhoods would still be expected to increase.

Furthermore, in what would have to be considered a worst case scenario, if a police subculture regarded the use of force as being more

---

[28] The use of force against some non-criminal individuals may be justified when police officers' must physically control or restrain individuals in altered mental or physical states (e.g., mentally or emotionally unstable, or under the influence of a controlled substance), but who have not committed any crimes. In such cases, if it is for the benefit of the individual, the police officer, or others, any reasonable amount of force necessary to control the situation should not be considered excessive, even if no crime has been committed.

justifiable in a broader range of circumstances, then members of that subculture might be expected to use force more often. Research has shown police subcultures to have a very powerful influence over officers' behaviors (Chappell and Piquero 2004; Micucci and Gomme 2005; Skolnick 1966; Terrill, Paoline, and Manning 2003; Waegel 1984a), so if the belief that people living in socially disorganized neighborhoods were more "deserving" of forceful behaviors (as Klinger's ecological theory of police vigor (1997) might contend – see review in Chapter 3), then officers might even come to believe that the use of excessive force was also *acceptable* in such neighborhoods. Consequently, if such pro-use-of-force beliefs spread throughout a department, then increased problems of police use of excessive force in disorganized neighborhoods would not be surprising.

Finally, regardless of why excessive force problems increase in socially disorganized neighborhoods, if officers began using overly excessive levels of force on residents (e.g., used deadly force against a misdemeanor offender), it is not expected that such behaviors go unnoticed or unpunished simply because they occurred in a socially disorganized neighborhood. Rather, the contention is that the "more common" abuses of force (e.g., unnecessary use of handcuffs, pressure holds, pain compliance techniques, impact maneuvers, etc.) would be most likely to increase when police officers realized that neighborhood residents would not anything to stop them. That is, unless an officer so grossly overstepped his or her use-of-force protocol that it somehow garnered attention from people outside of the neighborhood (e.g., severely beat a child or some other especially vulnerable individual), it would be unlikely that the residents of disorganized neighborhoods could prevent police officers' use of excessive force any more than they could prevent criminal activity.

Thus, for all the reasons discussed above, police officers are expected to use excessive levels of force more often in socially disorganized neighborhoods, where residents do not have the capacity to address the problem (i.e., low levels of social ties and/or collective efficacy), than in more organized neighborhoods. Unfortunately, data do not currently exist that assess police officers' perceptions of neighborhood social disorganization, so it is not yet possible to definitively test this theory. However, simply discovering whether objectively-defined social disorganization, and neighborhood collective efficacy in particular, is related to police use of excessive force is also very important.

Research Questions & Hypotheses

As reviewed earlier in this chapter, a small number of recent empirical studies provide some compelling evidence that aggregate-level contextual factors are related to police use of force behaviors (Kane 2002; Lawton 2007; Lersch et al. 2008; Terrill and Reisig 2003). To date, however, no research has convincingly demonstrated that the social disorganization tradition might be legitimately utilized as a theoretical framework for the study of police officers' use of excessive force. Thus, the primary goal of this book is to answer the broad question – *is neighborhood social disorganization related to police officers' use of excessive force?* Additionally, because most of the recent research testing concepts from the social disorganization tradition have found that the effect of neighborhood social ties (i.e., the systemic model) is not as consistent or powerful as the effect of neighborhood collective efficacy (see Chapter 2), this book more specifically attempts to answer the question – *is neighborhood collective efficacy a better predictor of police use of excessive force than other neighborhood contextual factors such as neighborhood structural disadvantage and social ties?*

In order to answer each of these research questions, it is essential that the relationships between each of the three most prominent concepts from the social disorganization tradition – neighborhood structural disadvantage, social ties, and collective efficacy – and police use of excessive force is examined. Although the latter two concepts are expected to mediate the relationship between the former concept and police officers' excessive force behaviors (as they have been shown to do for crime– see Chapter 2), it is first necessary to demonstrate that there is a relationship between neighborhood structural disadvantage and police use of force that can be mediated. Thus, the first hypothesis presented and discussed below pertains to the direct relationship between the three contextual factors that measure neighborhood structural disadvantage and police officers' use of excessive force.

Structural Disadvantage

As discussed in Chapter 3, social disorganization researchers understand that Shaw and McKay (1942) did not specifically posit a direct relationship between neighborhood structural disadvantage and crime. Despite this fact, however, the majority of studies testing concepts from the social disorganization tradition have continued to assess the direct effect of the three component measures of structural disadvantage – poverty, racial/ethnic heterogeneity, and residential instability. Following this precedent, the first hypothesis tested in this research predicts that each of the three component measures of structural disadvantage will be positively related to police officers' use of excessive force. Figure 4.1 below presents path diagrams for Hypotheses 1a through 1c.

Figure 4.1. Structural Disadvantage Hypotheses

Hypothesis 1a: Poverty (Direct Effect)

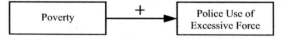

Hypothesis 1b: Racial/Ethnic Heterogeneity (Direct Effect)

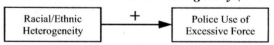

Hypothesis 1c: Residential Instability (Direct Effect)

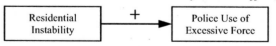

Systemic Model

Although recent research has begun to question the importance of neighborhood social ties (see Chapter 3), in order to fully test the social disorganization tradition as a framework for explaining police use of excessive force, it is necessary to propose and test a hypothesis based on the systemic model (Bursik and Grasmick 1993; Hunter 1985; Sampson and Groves 1989). And, even though some of that research has also been suggestive of a positive relationship between the number of neighborhood residents' social ties and crime (Bellair 1997; Browning et al. 2004; Patillo-McCoy 1999; Sampson et al. 1997; Wilson 1996), for this research, it is expected that larger social networks should still decrease police use of excessive force. This negative relationship is expected for two reasons. First, as systemic model theorists originally posited, as neighborhood social networks grow, it is expected that more people will care about the well-being of their neighbors, and then be willing to act on their behalf. Second, and most importantly, in the case of police use of excessive force, there should be no reason for neighborhood residents to cover up or shield the offending officers from punishment, as might be the case for well-networked criminals (see Chapter 3). It is therefore hypothesized that *neighborhood social ties will be negatively related to the police use of excessive force.* Figure 4.2 below presents the path diagram for Hypothesis 2a.

In addition to the direct relationship between the two phenomena, neighborhood social ties are also expected to mediate the relationship between neighborhood structural disadvantage and police use of excessive force. As reviewed in Chapter 3, the systemic model predicts that structural disadvantage will undermine neighborhood residents' ability to form strong social ties, which will then reduce residents' willingness to watch out for each other, and ultimately lead to an increase in crime rates. In regards to the police use of excessive force, a similar process of events is expected to occur. That is, neighborhood structural disadvantage should decrease the number of social ties among neighborhood residents, which should then lead them to be less likely to watch out, or care, for what happens to their neighbors. Ultimately, this process should result in an increase in police officers' use of excessive force since neighbors will not care about, or at the very least be unwilling to do anything about, incidents in which their neighbors are abused by the police. Thus, Hypothesis 2b states that neighborhood *social ties will mediate the relationship between neighborhood structural disadvantage and police officers' use of excessive force.*   Figure 4.2 below presents the path diagram for Hypothesis 2b.[29]

Figure 4.2. Systemic Model Hypotheses

Hypothesis 2a: Social Ties (Direct Effect)

Hypothesis 2b: Structural Disadvantage & Social Ties (Mediating Effect)

Collective Efficacy

The relationship between collective efficacy (Morenoff et al. 2001; Sampson et al. 1999; Sampson et al. 1997) and police officers' use of excessive force is the primary focus of this book. A large body of research has shown that collective efficacy is a strong, robust, predictor of neighborhood crime rates (see Chapter 3). A similar relationship is expected between collective efficacy and police use of excessive force. Specifically, it is expected that neighborhoods with low social cohesion (i.e., mutual trust and solidarity) and low informal social control (i.e.,

---

[29] To conserve space, the three components of poverty, racial/ethnic heterogeneity, and residential instability, will be collectively depicted as "structural disadvantage" in the remaining path diagrams. However, as with Hypotheses 1a – 1c, the effects of all three components will be analyzed separately in order to determine the individual effects of each component of structural disadvantage on the mediating and dependent variables. Thus, in each of the remaining path diagrams presented in this chapter, it is expected that all three components of structural disadvantage will have the same relationship (directionally) with the variable(s) they are predicting.

willingness to intervene for the common good of the neighborhood) will be unable to come together as a group and put a stop to police officers' use of excessive force. The first collective efficacy hypothesis tested in this book therefore states that *neighborhood collective efficacy will be negatively related to police officers' use of excessive force.* Figure 4.3 below presents the path diagram for Hypothesis 3a.

As with the systemic model discussed above, the level of neighborhood collective efficacy is also expected to mediate the relationship between structural disadvantage and the police use of excessive force. That is, as increases in neighborhood structural disadvantage make it difficult for residents to come together and find a common set of goals and values, they will never come to trust those neighbors to intervene on the behalf of the neighborhood. Ultimately, just as social disorganization researchers believe that this lack of collective efficacy signals to criminals that they can get away with committing crimes, the same processes should also signal to police officers that they too can get away with inappropriate behaviors, including the use of excessive force. Thus, it is also hypothesized that *collective efficacy will mediate the relationship between neighborhood structural disadvantage and police officers' use of excessive force.* Figure 4.3 below presents the path diagram for Hypothesis 3b.

Figure 4.3. Collective Efficacy Hypotheses

Hypothesis 3a: Collective Efficacy (Direct Effect)

Hypothesis 3b: Structural Disadvantage & Collective Efficacy (Mediating Effect)

<u>Systemic Model vs. Collective Efficacy</u>

While the overall goal of this book is to establish a relationship between neighborhood social disorganization and police officers' use of excessive force, it also seeks to answer the more specific research question – *is neighborhood collective efficacy the best predictor of police use of excessive force, net of other neighborhood contextual factors such as neighborhood structural disadvantage and neighborhood social ties?* Collective efficacy is expected to be the best (i.e., strongest and most robust) predictor of police officers' use of excessive force for two reasons. First, a number of recent empirical tests of the systemic model have suggested that relationship between social ties and criminal activity could actually be both positive and negative (Bellair 1997; Browning et al. 2004; Patillo-McCoy 1999; Sampson et al. 1997; Wilson 1996). Second, in the only extant study to simultaneously examine the effect of social ties and collective efficacy on neighborhood crime rates, Browning and colleagues (2004) found that collective efficacy was the better predictor, net of a series of controls. As a result of these studies, it is likely that collective efficacy may be the best predictor of not only crime rates, but also neighborhood problems with police officers' use of excessive force. [30]

To put it more clearly, the mutual trust shared by neighbors to engage in informal social control behaviors (i.e., collective efficacy) is expected to be the most important factor for reducing both problems with crime and problems with police use of excessive force, even in neighborhoods where residents do not know each other well (i.e., do not share close social ties). To wit, Sampson and colleagues once

---

[30] Although there is some reason to believe that it might (for a discussion see Sampson et al. 1999), collective efficacy is not expected to mediate the relationship between social ties and the police use of excessive force. Instead, for the purposes of this research, the systemic model and the collective efficacy framework are considered to be competing explanations of both crime and police use of excessive force. Subsequently, no hypotheses regarding a mediation effect are tested here. Instead, it is simply expected that collective efficacy will be the more powerful and robust predictor of police officers' use of excessive force, net of the effect of neighborhood social ties.

similarly argued that "[collective efficacy] facilitates social control without requiring strong social ties or associations" (Morenoff et al. 2001:250). Accordingly, in neighborhoods where residents trust their neighbors to exercise informal social control when necessary and regardless of the strength of their ties to those neighbors, it is expected that there will be fewer problems not only with crime, but with police use of excessive force as well. The fourth and final hypothesis tested in this research therefore states that *neighborhood collective efficacy will be the strongest and most robust predictor of officers' use of excessive force, net of all the other social disorganization tradition measures.* Figure 4.4 below presents the path diagram for Hypothesis 4.

Figure 4.4. Full Social Disorganization Tradition Hypothesis

Hypothesis 4: Comparative Effects

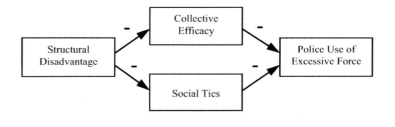

CHAPTER 5

Testing a Social Disorganization Theory of Police Use of Force

In order to determine the viability of the social disorganization tradition as a theoretical framework for explaining police use of force, it is necessary to assess whether, and how much, measures of various concepts from the tradition are empirically related to each other. As reviewed in the previous chapter, all of the existing research examining social disorganization concepts and police use of force has suffered from serious flaws. There are four primary ways in which the research conducted in this book improves upon past research and contributes to our better understanding of police use of force.

First and foremost, this is the first study to actually formulate a new theory of police use of force (see Chapter 3) and empirically test it. Second, previous research on the subject has tested only one, or at most two, measures of structural disadvantage. The goal of this study is to precisely operationalize and then test all of the major neighborhood contextual processes that characterize the social disorganization tradition, including neighborhood structural disadvantage, social ties, and collective efficacy, many of which have yet to be examined. Third, prior research testing aggregate-level predictors of police use of force have, for the most part, either not actually tested *neighborhood* effects, or have done so poorly (e.g., using census tracts or police districts). A primary emphasis of this research is the accurate measurement of true neighborhoods so that a discussion of "neighborhood contextual effects" can actually mean just that. Finally, even though some past research has utilized multi-level modeling techniques, none have done so to the full extent that they could, and really should, have. The analyses conducted herein consider both individual-level measures to account for neighborhood compositional effects as well as the aforementioned neighborhood contextual effects that are the primary focus of this study.[31]

---

[31] A more detailed discussion of the differences between neighborhood compositional and contextual effects can be found later in this chapter.

Data

Data that can accurately measure both social disorganization tradition concepts and police use of force is extremely rare, and may be one reason that so little research has been conducted in the area. Fortunately, the primary source of data for this research is the Community Survey portion of the Project on Human Development in Chicago Neighborhoods (PHDCN: Earls et al. 1997) which also just so happens to be the same data source that Sampson and colleagues (Morenoff et al. 2001; Sampson et al. 1999; Sampson et al. 1997) utilized to first create their concept of collective efficacy. As such, the Community Survey portion of the PHDCN is an ideal source of data for this study. Not only did it capture the concept of collective efficacy (i.e., neighborhood informal social control and social cohesion) just as its creators intended, it also measured respondents' number of social ties (i.e., the systemic model) and their perceptions of police officers' use of excessive force. In addition to these essential measures, the PHDCN also contains a number of individual-level demographic characteristics that will allow me to control for neighborhood compositional effects as well as a variety of factors that may potentially influence respondents' reports of police officers' use of excessive force.[32]

The Community Survey portion of the PHDCN was originally conducted by Earls and colleagues between 1994 and 1995. Survey data come from in-home interviews of randomly selected Chicago residents 18 years of age and older. Surveyors used a three-stage sampling process to identify respondents throughout the entire city of Chicago. First, they sampled city blocks within neighborhood clusters (defined in more detail below), then dwelling units within each city block, and finally one adult resident within each sampled dwelling unit. The response rate for the survey was 75%, and the final sample size used for analysis was 8,765 respondents (of a possible 8,782) within 342 (of a possible 343) neighborhood clusters. On average, 26 respondents were surveyed within each neighborhood cluster (ranging

---

[32] More on how civilian reporting bias is accounted for in this research can be found below.

from a minimum of 8 respondents to a maximum of 62 respondents). Of the individuals surveyed, a slight majority were female (59%), most were racial or ethnic minorities (white 27%; black 40%; Hispanic 26%; Asian 3%; other race category 5%), nearly 60% had only a high school education or less (only a third of respondents had completed a four-year college degree, and less than 10% had graduate degrees), and approximately half of the respondents reported annual family incomes of under $25,000 (only 11% made more than $60,000 a year, and less than 2% made over $100,000). For more information on the Community Survey portion of the PHDCN, the original data, codebook, and survey instrument are available from the Inter-university Consortium for Political and Social Research (ICPSR).

What Does Neighborhood Really Mean?

Within the PHDCN, neighborhood clusters (referred to simply as "neighborhoods" for the remainder of this book) were defined as geographically contiguous and socially homogenous communities (with respect to racial/ethnic composition, social class composition, housing density, and family structure) that took into consideration major geographic boundaries (e.g., railroad tracks, parks, freeways, etc.) as well as the researchers' knowledge of Chicago's local neighborhood structure (Sampson et al. 1997; Morenoff et al. 2001).[33] 343 neighborhoods containing approximately 8,000 individuals each were identified. These neighborhoods serve as the unit of analysis for this study. Although the operationalization of "neighborhoods" in the PHDCN is intended to be "as ecologically meaningful as possible" (Sampson et. al 1997:919), it is nonetheless important to consider how previous neighborhoods and crime researchers have defined and operationalized the concept.

Researchers studying neighborhoods have long debated how to best define and operationalize their primary units of analysis. The way in which they did so could have profound implications for the interpretation of neighborhood contextual effects in which they were so interested. Should researchers use "real world" definitions based on

---

[33] Each of the original PHDCN: Community Survey researchers either lived or worked in Chicago (primarily at the University of Chicago) during the period in which it was administered and have extensive knowledge of the city.

residents' perceptions of their own neighborhood's boundaries, or could such definitions be too subjective? Should they rely on governmental demarcations that are based primarily on population size rather than any substantive factors of interest, or could such definitions be too objective? Or, should researchers create their own definitions based on the specific areas and types of phenomena that they were primarily interested in studying, as was done in the PHDCN? Unfortunately, to this day, there are no definitive answers to these questions.

While gathering data on residents' perceptions of their neighborhoods' boundaries might allow for a better "real world" operationalization, getting such information requires specific studies of certain locales, and cannot be used to make comparisons to, or broad generalizations about, other neighborhoods outside the area being studied. That is, while residents may be able to better identify the spatial (e.g., streets, buildings, or other physical landmarks) and social (e.g., the distance to friends and family) indicators that separate their own neighborhood from someone else's neighborhood, those indicators could not be applied to other places. Additionally, past research has shown that residents' perceptions of their neighborhood's boundaries can vary based on a variety of social and demographic characteristics, including age, sex, race, and social class (Lee and Campbell 1997). For example, in their study of Nashville neighborhoods, Lee and Campbell (1997) found that black residents were more likely than white residents to define their neighborhoods through the use of social, rather than spatial, indicators and as being smaller in general. Thus, the use of residents' perceptions to define and operationalize neighborhood boundaries can be problematic.

The use of government-defined boundaries, on the other hand, involves its own set of advantages and disadvantages. The most commonly used government-defined boundaries come from the U.S. Census Bureau in the form of census tracts.[34] The primary advantage of using census tracts as proxies for neighborhoods is the widespread

---

[34] Census tract boundaries are defined based on population size and are intended to encompass areas in which there approximately 4,000 residents (U.S. Census Bureau 1997).

availability of decennial data on a variety of demographic and housing-related topics across the nation. Subsequently, researchers using census tracts as their units of analysis are able to compare "neighborhoods" in many different locations and make broader generalizations about the results they observe. However, while use of census tract boundaries as proxies for actual neighborhood boundaries has generally been accepted by both ecological and criminological researchers (e.g., Morenoff et al. 1997; South and Crowder 1997), such artificial, population-based boundary definitions may not accurately reflect the boundaries in which researchers' phenomena of interest truly operate (Tienda 1991). Consequently, census tracts boundaries may not actually encompass the same geographic area that the average resident might call his or her "neighborhood." Even so, in the absence of widely available data sources that use more substantive definitions to create uniform neighborhood boundaries, the use of census tracts as proxies for neighborhoods is more the rule than the exception.

The final alternative for identifying neighborhood boundaries is to take the route chosen in the PHDCN. Rather than interviewing individuals and attempting to define neighborhood boundaries based on the reports of actual residents, or using population-based governmental demarcations, researchers can also use a combination of the two approaches. In the case of the PHDCN, researchers used individuals' knowledge of Chicago (their own and that of Chicago city planners), spatial indicators (i.e., natural and manmade geographic boundaries), and census-based social indicators (cluster analyses using a variety of demographic characteristics were conducted by the primary investigators [Earls et al. 1997] to verify their results).

Unfortunately, however, as with the use of neighborhood residents' perceptions, the use of a mixed methods approach utilized in the PHDCN makes the resulting data location-specific to only the city and neighborhoods of Chicago. Nonetheless, since the PHDCN is currently one of the only existing studies that has obtained information on both neighborhood contextual processes (i.e., social disorganization) and police use of (any type of) force, it remains an ideal data source for this research. Moreover, the precedent for using PHDCN-defined neighborhoods has been set by a number of well-known and well-respected criminological researchers (e.g., Sampson et al. 1997; Sampson et al. 1999; Morenoff et al. 1997). Subsequently, this research, unlike most of the related studies reviewed in Chapter 4 (Kane 2002; Lawton 2007; Lersch et al. 2008), should provide much more valid and reliable estimates of *neighborhood*-contextual effects on police use of force.

Measuring Police Use of *Excessive* Force

The dependent variable tested in this research is PHDCN respondents' perceptions of police officers' use of excessive force in their neighborhoods. Respondents were asked whether they believed that police officers' use of excessive force was "not a problem," "somewhat of a problem," or "a big problem?" As might be expected, the smallest percentage of residents reported "big" problems of police use of excessive force (7%), while slightly more (11%) reported that it was "somewhat of a problem." Most residents (82%) reported that police use of excessive force was "not a problem" at all.

Regrettably, the original PHDCN researchers provided no objective definition of "excessive" force to the respondents. As a consequence, how respondents responded to the question posed to them may have been dependent on two other questions that were not asked: 1) what does "force" mean to each respondent (i.e., some individuals might have perceived verbal threats to be "force," while others perceived only physical contact to be "force"), and 2) at what threshold does the use of force become excessive (i.e., some individuals might have perceived higher levels of force to be justified in certain cases, while others may have perceived the same amount of force to be unjustified in the same, or similar, cases)? Unfortunately, it is beyond the scope of this research to empirically assess how individuals define "force" or at what threshold force becomes "excessive."[35] Fortunately, however, as discussed below, considerable efforts are made in this research to eliminate any potential measurement error in the dependent variable that may be due to systematic civilian reporting biases.

Before describing the primary explanatory variables used for this research, it is important to briefly review how the results of the

---

[35] Such research could fill a glaring hole in the police use of force literature and should be considered an vital avenue for future research.

analyses presented later in this book (see Chapter 6) should be interpreted. First, it should be noted that although the dependent variable is measured at the individual-level, responses are analyzed at the neighborhood-level. Thus, neighborhood differences in the average reported level of police use of excessive force serve as the primary outcome of interest. Additionally, because the survey question posed to the PHDCN respondents was not continuous in nature, ordinal regression analysis is utilized for this research. Subsequently, the results of these analyses reveal whether or not any of the explanatory variables described below *increase or decrease the odds that excessive force will be more of a problem in a neighborhood.*

The Issue of Civilian Reporting Bias

While the primary objective of this research is to observe a relationship between concepts from the social disorganization tradition and *actual police behavior*, as reviewed above, the dependent variable that is analyzed herein captures only *civilians' perceptions of police use of excessive force.* Unfortunately, the use of civilian reports of police behavior is problematic. Fortunately, however, there are three compelling reasons to believe that civilians' perceptions of police behaviors can be used to accurately determine the relationship between neighborhood social disorganization and police officers' actual use of excessive force.

First, previous research suggests that the use of civilian reports in the study of police officers' behaviors provides results that can be just as accurate and reliable as the two other commonly utilized sources of data on police behavior – *police officer self-report surveys* and *systematic observational data* (e.g., Parks 1982, 1984; Percy 1986; Son and Rome 2004). A common sense approach to critiquing civilian reports of police behaviors might suggest that both police officer self-report and systematic observational data should be more accurate and reliable sources of data on police behavior. The general argument against the use of civilian surveys is that their reports of police behavior may be biased for, or against, the police.

For example, if the spouse of a police officer was surveyed, he or she might provide a more positive report of police officers' behaviors based on his or her general attitude toward the police. If a person with a history of negative experiences with the police was surveyed, on the other hand, he or she might provide a more negative report of police behavior based on a generally more negative view of the police. Based on this type of reasoning, some might then argue that police officer self-reports and systematic observational data should be more accurate and reliable since actual officers and trained observers are reporting on the behaviors in which they have engaged or personally observed, respectively. Interestingly, however, there is persuasive evidence that both types of data may be no more accurate or reliable than civilian surveys, such as the PHDCN.

In an early study specifically intended to compare all three forms of data on police behavior, Parks (1982) found that police officers often report their own deviant behaviors inaccurately (including the use of excessive force) because they "face some incentives to record information that reflects favorably upon them, to the detriment of accurate recording" (1982:20). In fact, Parks concluded that there was actually a high level agreement between citizens' and trained observers' reports, and that police officer self-reports were "the primary locus of measurement error" in studies of police misconduct (1982:20). He also concluded that some police officers alter their behaviors in the presence of an observer so that even observational data may not be as accurate a reflection of "real-life" decisions or actions as many might believe. Thus, according to at least one researcher, "the evidence is not strong against the use of citizen reports" (1982:24).

More recent studies have further supported the argument that civilian reports can provide accurate and reliable data for the study of actual police use of force behaviors. Percy (1986) concluded that civilians' and police officers' evaluations of police actions were "roughly consistent" (1986:80). Mastrofski and Parks (1990) found that some officers admitted to altering their behavior when an observer was present. Spano and Reisig (2006; see also Spano 2005, 2006) came to a similar conclusion when they observed trained observers becoming involved in police officer-civilian encounters which ultimately altered the outcome of events. Finally, in their examination of police officer misconduct (including the use of excessive force), Son and Rome (2004) found that officers reported higher levels of misconduct by their fellow police officers than did civilians (see also,

Micucci and Gomme 2005). All together, these studies suggest that, in comparison to police self-report and systematic observational data, civilian reports may also be accurate and reliable resources for studying police use of force.[36]

The second reason to be confident that the respondents' perceptions of police use of excessive force in the PHDCN are both accurate and reliable is that average level of reported excessive force problems are utilized as the dependent variable Because the perceptions of many respondents within each neighborhood are used, the neighborhood mean level of police officers' use of excessive force is more likely to correspond with the true level of the behavior than would the perceptions of any one respondent (for a similar argument, see Silver and Miller 2004). That is, even if a small number of respondents make inaccurate or biased reports about the problem of police use of excessive force in their neighborhoods, by analyzing the average of all respondents' reports, those inaccurate or biased reports should be evened out. Thus, when taking into account the accuracy and reliability of civilian reports in comparison to other potential data sources on police behavior *and* the fact that the dependent variable for this research is each neighborhood's average level of excessive force as reported by its residents, only one reason for concern regarding the accuracy of the dependent variable analyzed for this research remains – systematic (i.e., non-random) bias related to neighborhood differences in the sample characteristics of the PHDCN.

A large body of research has found that there is in fact a systematic pattern of bias in regards to civilians' perceptions of the police. Although this research does not specifically link perceptions of the police to inaccurate reporting of police use of excessive force, a

---

[36] In each of the studies discussed here (Parks 1982, 1984; Percy 1986; Son and Rome 2004), it should be noted that the researchers were comparing civilians' *observations* of actual police behaviors to the observations of other police officers and trained observers. The data for the dependent variable measuring problems with police officers' use of excessive force *may* also capture some respondents' actual observations of the use of excessive force by the police, but it very likely also captures respondents' perceptions of problems that were not based on direct observations (i.e., perceptions based on vicarious reports of police use of excessive force related to them by other individuals).

number of studies by Weitzer and colleagues (Weitzer 1999, 2002; Weitzer and Tuch 2004) have all found that many of the same factors that influence citizens' perceptions of the police also influence citizens' reports of police misconduct. Subsequently, because it is one form of police misconduct, it is reasonable to expect that those factors that influence civilians' reports of police misconduct in general might also influence their reports of police use of excessive force in particular. Fortunately, however, the third and final reason to be confident in the use of the PHDCN data in this study is that the findings of past research can be used to identify and then account for any potential civilian reporting bias in this research.

How Perceptions of the Police Influence Civilian Reports

Civilians' perceptions of the police are one of the most studied topics in the field of policing research (for reviews see Brown and Benedict [2002] and Decker [1981]). Over the last fifty years, researchers have identified a number of individual-level factors, and at least one aggregate-level factor, that have the potential to influence how civilians perceive the police. For the purposes of this research, a review of these factors can help determine what variables should be included in the later analyses to account for any bias that PHDCN respondents might have had for or against the police (and which might have influenced their reports of police officers' behavior). If those factors can then be included in the analyses, their effects can be statistically controlled, thereby leaving only the estimated effects of the various social disorganization tradition concepts that are the central focus of this book. In other words, if all of the factors that may lead to civilian reporting bias can be held constant, the true effects of the explanatory variables on variation in police officers' use of excessive force can be observed, net of those biasing factors. Consequently, understanding what factors are the most likely to influence civilians' perceptions of the police is essential to this research.

Perhaps the most consistent finding of researchers examining civilians' perception of the police is that poor, young, minorities, with negative previous contacts with the police, and who live in high crime neighborhoods are the most likely to have negative views of the police.[37]   And, of those five factors, an individual's race or ethnic background appears to be the most important. Since the 1960s, dozens of studies have shown that racial/ethnic minorities, and especially blacks, tend to hold more negative views of the police in comparison to whites (e.g., Bordua and Tifft 1971; Hagan and Albonetti 1982; Reisig and Parks 2000; Sampson and Jeglum-Bartusch 1998; Tuch and Weitzer 1997; Webb and Marshall 1995).   Other research has also shown that, in comparison to whites, racial/ethnic minorities, and once again, blacks in particular, are less likely to approve of police uses of force, which is in turn related to more negative perceptions of the police as well (e.g., Elicker 2008; Halim and Stiles 2001; Johnson, Devon, and Kuhns 2009; Thompson and Lee 2004).

Many studies have also found that lower-class individuals are more likely to have negative view of the police compared to upper- and middle-class individuals (e.g., Cao, Frank, and Cullen 1996; Jacob 1971; Marenin 1983; Percy 1980; Sampson and Jeglum-Bartusch 1998). In regards to age, research has shown that younger individuals tend to view the police less favorably than do older individuals (e.g., Cao et al. 1996; Hadar and Snortum 1975; Kaminski and Jefferis 1998; Sampson and Jeglum-Bartusch 1998; Webb and Marshall 1995; Worrall 1999).   And, not surprisingly, a majority of research on individuals' previous contacts with the police has also shown that those with direct previous negative experiences (e.g., being arrested, questioned, or physically or verbally abused by the police) are the most likely to hold negative views of the police, compared to those with more positive experiences (e.g., officers responded to a request for help or helped to resolve a problem), or those with no direct positive or negative experiences (e.g., hearing stories of other people's experiences) (e.g., Bordua and Tifft 1971; Jacob 1971; Weitzer and Tuch 2005; Worrall 1999).

Finally, there have been a handful of studies that have found a neighborhood-level contextual effect on perceptions of the police. Most of this research has focused on the effect of living in a high crime

---

[37] The effect of another commonly-studied demographic characteristic, gender, on perceptions of the police is less clear. See discussion below.

neighborhood.[38]   Specifically, these studies have indicated that individuals living in neighborhoods with high rates of crime tend to have greater fear of being victimized, and subsequently, also tend to view the police in a more negative light (e.g., Cao et al. 1996; Davis 1990; Percy 1986; Reisig and Giacomazzi 1998; Sampson and Jeglum-Bartusch 1998; Weitzer and Tuch 2005).

In addition to the five factors described above, a number of studies have also considered what influence individual-level factors such as gender and past criminal victimization may have. The findings of this research are inconsistent at best, however. In regards to gender, some researchers have found that males hold more negative views of the police (Cao et al. 1996; Hadar and Snortum 1975; Reisig and Giacomazzi 1998), while others have found that females hold more negative views (Correia, Reisig, and Lovrich 1996; Elicker 2008; Halim and Stiles 2001; Thompson and Lee 2004), and still others have found no gender effect at all (Marenin 1983; Murty, Roebuck, and Smith 1990; Percy 1980; Sampson and Jeglum-Bartusch 1998; Thurman and Reisig 1996; Worrall 1999). In regards to past criminal victimization experiences, results have been similarly inconsistent. Some researchers have found that individuals who have been victimized in the past tend to hold more negative views of the police (Carter 1985; Homant, Kennedy, and Fleming 1984), while at least one pair of researchers found that victims actually held more positive views (Thurman and Reisig 1996), and yet another pair found no effect of past victimization at all (Smith and Hawkins 1973).

---

[38] Some studies have considered the effect of living in different areas (e.g., census tracts, neighborhoods, cities, etc.) on perceptions of the police. Unfortunately, these studies have not clearly specified which aspects of living in different those areas are expected to influence residents' perceptions of the police (e.g., Cao et al. 1996; Jacob 1971; Murty et al. 1990). Furthermore, in two studies examining neighborhood-level compositional factors (i.e., racial/ethnic and social class compositions), Weitzer (1999, 2000) found that when controlling for their individual-level counterparts, neighborhood-level effects disappeared. It is therefore still unclear what effect neighborhood characteristics have on civilians' perceptions of the police.

Accounting for Reporting Bias

As reviewed above, there are a number of important factors that researchers have linked to civilian perceptions of the police. Although there is compelling evidence that civilian reports of police behavior can be just as accurate as police officer self-reports or systematic observational data (Parks 1982, 1984; Percy 1986; Son and Rome 2004), it is still important to account for any potential variation in those reports that may be due to reporting bias associated with civilians' perceptions of the police. As luck would have it, the Community Survey portion of the PHDCN includes measures of many of the individual-level civilian reporting bias factors discussed above (e.g., race, age, gender, social class, and criminal victimization) and data from the Chicago Police Department on neighborhood-level crime rates is also available for inclusion in the empirical analyses (discussed in more detail below).

Data for ten individual-level civilian reporting bias controls come from the PHDCN. The dichotomous variable *male* measures respondents' gender, where male = 1 and female = 0. Respondents' *social class* is measured using a principal components factor analysis of each respondents' highest level of education attained, annual family income, and occupational prestige (for precedent, see Sampson et al. 1997; Sampson et al. 1999; Morenoff et al. 1997). Respondents' *age* was calculated by subtracting their reported birthdates from the year the study was conducted (1994). The resulting number was then divided by ten in order to ease interpretation and maintain a similar metric with the other variables included in analyses. Respondents' *race/ethnicity* was measured using five mutually exclusive dichotomous variables assessing the category that best represented their racial/ethnic background – white, black, Hispanic, Asian, or other.[39] Finally, respondents' *past criminal victimization* is measured using a scale of

---

[39] Because research has identified racial/ethnic minorities as being more likely to hold negative views of the police, for the purposes of this research, whites are used as the reference category. Therefore, in the analytic models discussed below, only the four minority group measures are included for testing, results should be interpreted as the effect of being in a particular racial/ethnic group in comparison to being white.

four dichotomous items assessing whether or not they have ever been the victim of physical assault (including sexual assaults), burglary, larceny, or vandalism. The individual-level mean for the past criminal victimization variable was 0.87, indicating that the average respondent had not experienced any criminal victimization in the past ($\alpha = 0.54$).

Unfortunately, the PHDCN does not include any direct measures of respondents' previous contacts with the police. However, in order to capture some of the variation in the dependent variable that might be attributable to bias associated with previous contacts with the police, a scale measure of respondents' general feelings of legal cynicism is included. Respondents' *legal cynicism* is comprised of five items assessing how much they agreed or disagreed with statements regarding whether it was okay 1) to break the law, 2) do whatever they wanted as long no one got hurt, 3) to believe that there was no right or wrong way to make money, 4) to consider domestic fighting to be a private matter, and 5) live for the day. Respondents were given the following response options, based on a 5-item Likert-type scale: strongly agree, agree, neither agree nor disagree, disagree, or strongly disagree. The individual-level mean for legal cynicism was 2.35, indicating that the average respondent very slightly disagreed with all of the statements relating to legal cynicism ($\alpha = 0.65$). Although respondents' legal cynicism does not directly measure their past contacts with the police, the concept is likely to be related to their positive or negative views of the police. Additionally, the victimization variable discussed above may also capture some of the variation in the dependent variable that might be due to reporting bias associated with previous police contacts.[40]

---

[40] Items forming a scalar measure of respondents' satisfaction with the police are also available in the PHDCN, but are not included in analyses because of their high correlation with the dependent variable ($r = -0.78$, $p < 0.000$), and the unclear causal relationship. While it is possible that respondents' satisfaction with the police may lead to reporting bias affecting the dependent variable, past research has also shown that police use of excessive force influences individuals' satisfaction with the police (e.g., Son, Tsang, Rome, and Davis 1997). While the same argument might be applied to respondents' more general feelings of legal cynicism, that measure was not as strongly correlated

In addition to the nine (ten, including the dichotomous variable measuring "white" as the race/ethnicity reference category) civilian reporting bias controls discussed above, two more individual-level control variables using data from the PHDCN are included in the analyses that follow. Respondents' *marital status* is a dichotomous variable, where married = 1 and unmarried = 0 (including never married, divorced, and widowed). Respondents' *mobility* is a continuous measure assessing the number of household moves that they have made over the past five years. Although there is no previous research that has linked either marital status or the number of moves to civilian reporting bias, married individuals and those who have not moved often may be more settled in a neighborhood, may have had more interactions with the police, and may better know the police officers who work there, for better or worse. Therefore, because both variables have the potential to influence respondents' reports of police behavior, they are included to round out the individual-level civilian reporting bias control variables included in this study.

The final civilian reporting bias control variable included in analyses below is a neighborhood-level measure of crime rates. For this research, only neighborhood homicide rates are examined, because measures of other crime rates for the PHDCN-defined neighborhoods are not available. This is not necessarily a problem however. Although the inclusion of other crime rate measures (e.g., non-homicide-violent crime, property crime, or total crime) might be desirable, criminologists generally agree that data on homicides is the most accurately reported and reliably recorded (Biderman and Lynch 1991; Gove, Hughes, and Geerken 1985; O'Brien 1985). Thus, for the purposes of this research, homicide rates will serve as proxies for crime in general.[41] Data for the homicide rates (per 100,000 population) variable come from the Chicago Police Department between 1991 and 1993 and are geo-coded

---

with the dependent variable (r = 0.24, p <0.000). Thus, because of the strong correlation with police use of excessive force and the unclear causal sequencing, the scale of satisfaction with the police is not included in any of the following analyses.

[41] See also Morenoff et al. (1997); Sampson et al. (1997); Sampson et al. (1999); Sampson et al. (2001); Sampson et al. (2002) for precedent.

to match neighborhood boundaries as they are defined by the PHDCN.[42]

All together, 12 individual- and neighborhood-level civilian reporting bias controls are included in the analyses that follow.[43] If the results of this research reveal that concepts from the social disorganization tradition are indeed related to police use of excessive force, net of these 12 controls, it will be reasonable to conclude that variation in actual police behaviors has been captured, rather than change in respondents' perceptions of the police.

Neighborhood Social Disorganization

In order to determine whether or not neighborhood social disorganization is empirically related to police officers' use of excessive force, five neighborhood-level explanatory variables from the social disorganization tradition – concentrated disadvantage,

---

[42] While many of the variables discussed in this section might be alternatively used to compare the capacity of a social disorganization explanation of police officers' use of force to social threat or criminal threat explanations, because the primary focus of this research is to come as close as possible to explaining actual police behavior, those variables that might also be used to measure other theories are instead used to account for civilian reporting bias. Implications of this study for the social threat and criminal threat theories are addressed in the final chapter of this research.

[43] Although including a variety of neighborhood-level compositional control variables is possible using the PHDCN data (i.e., including neighborhood means of each individual-level control variable), the effect of neighborhood composition on individuals' perceptions of the police is unclear. As reviewed above, with the exception of racial/ethnic and social class composition, there has been no research examining neighborhood compositional effects. And, the research that does examine racial/ethnic and social class compositional effects has generally found that those effects disappear when controlling for their individual-level counterparts (see Weitzer 1999, 2000). Thus, no additional neighborhood-level compositional effects are included in the analyses conducted in this research.

concentrated immigration, residential instability, social ties, and collective efficacy – are included in the following analyses.

Unlike the rest of the social disorganization explanatory variables listed above, data for neighborhood concentrated disadvantage, concentrated immigration, and residential instability come from the 1990 U.S. Census of Population and Housing. Although the names and operationalization of these variables are not entirely consistent with the three measures of neighborhood structural disadvantage identified by Shaw and McKay (1942) and discussed in Chapter 3 (poverty, racial/ethnic heterogeneity, and residential mobility), they do capture the same three structural factors that lead to neighborhood social disorganization. Subsequently, for the remainder of this book, neighborhood concentrated disadvantage, concentrated immigration, and residential instability are collectively referred to as neighborhood structural disadvantage. In fact, all three variables have been used in a similar fashion by previous social disorganization researchers (Morenoff 2001; Sampson et al. 1997; Sampson et al. 1999). Each variable was constructed using factor loadings (from a factor analysis of nine census items using alpha scoring and oblique rotation) as weights, which were then used to create the concentrated disadvantage, concentrated immigration, and residential instability summary scales.[44]

The *concentrated disadvantage* factor is comprised of the neighborhood percentage of 1) families living in poverty, 2) percentage of families receiving public assistance (i.e., welfare), 3) percentage individuals unemployed, 4) percentage black, and 5) percentage female-headed households with children. The *concentrated immigration* factor is comprised of two census characteristics, neighborhood percentage 1) Hispanic and 2) foreign-born. Finally, the *residential instability* factor is comprised of two census characteristics,

---

[44] As briefly discussed earlier in this chapter, the level of aggregation in the PHDCN is the neighborhood, as defined by the original researchers. Census data is not available at this study-specific aggregation, however, Sampson and colleagues (1997) were able to geo-code census tracts to match the original researchers' "neighborhood clusters." Therefore, even though all three structural disadvantage factors were created using census tract data, they have been adjusted to fit the PHDCN's, and therefore this book's, definition of neighborhood.

neighborhood percentage 1) rented homes and 2) residents not living in the same home in 1985. And, because each of the above factors generally measures the same neighborhood structural characteristics identified by Shaw and McKay (1942), for the purposes of this research, neighborhood concentrated disadvantage serves as a proxy for neighborhood poverty and concentrated immigration serves as a proxy for racial/ethnic heterogeneity, while residential instability closely matches what the theorists originally intended. As explained in Chapter 4, each measure is expected to predict police officers' use of excessive force in the same way it has been found to predict crime. That is, each factor should be positively related to police officers' use of excessive force.[45]

The remaining two neighborhood-level explanatory variables from the social disorganization tradition are 1) neighborhood social ties (i.e., the systemic model) and 2) the combination of neighborhood informal social control and neighborhood social cohesion (i.e., collective efficacy). Data for each variable come from the Community Survey portion of the PHDCN, and each variable is a scalar measures comprised of the neighborhood mean level of z-scores for a variety of aggregated individual-level items (see Sampson et al. 1997; Sampson et al. 1999).[46] Descriptive statistics for the neighborhood social ties and

---

[45] As discussed in Chapter 4, in order to determine which factor might drive the relationship between structural disadvantage and police officers' use of excessive force, the three factors used to measure neighborhood structural disadvantage (concentrated disadvantage, concentrated immigration, and residential instability) are analyzed separately, rather than as a combined scale or latent variable.

[46] All of the neighborhood-level explanatory variables using PHDCN data were constructed using the neighborhood-level mean of all the respondents' individual-level survey responses. In an ecometric analysis of their similarly constructed neighborhood-level measures, Raudenbush and Sampson (1999) found that having approximately 20 respondents in each neighborhood produced sufficiently high enough levels of reliability. As described earlier in this chapter, there was an average of 26 respondents per neighborhood, so it safe to conclude that the neighborhood social ties and neighborhood collective

neighborhood collective efficacy scales are presented in Chapter 6. The original survey instruments for each item utilized here are presented in the Appendix at the end of the book.

For the *neighborhood social ties* variable, a scale comprised of two items assessing the mean number of close relationships that respondents had with other residents of their neighborhood was created (for precedent, see Morenoff et al. 2001). Specifically, respondents were asked to identify the number of 1) family members (including in-laws) and 2) friends they had in their neighborhood, and were given the following response options: no family or friends, one or two, three to five, six to nine, or ten or more. Combined, the items in this scale measure the average number of close social relationships (i.e., social ties) that respondents shared within a neighborhood. The individual-level mean number of friends and family members was 2.56, indicating that the average respondent had one to five close relationships with others in their neighborhood ($\alpha = 0.42$).[47] This variable is used to test the systemic model approach of the social disorganization tradition. As discussed in Chapters 3, based on empirical tests of the systemic model, it is difficult to predict what effect neighborhood social ties will have on police officers' use of excessive force behavior. Nevertheless, as outlined in Chapter 4, it is expected that neighborhood social ties should be negatively related to police use of excessive force.

The *neighborhood collective efficacy* scale actually consists of two other scales and was calculated using the neighborhood-level means of all the z-scores for the respondents in each neighborhood. Data again come from the Community Survey portion of the PHDCN. Four items measure *neighborhood informal social control*. Respondents were asked how likely they believed their neighbors would be to intervene

---

efficacy variables included in this study are in fact reliable measures of the actual phenomena.

[47] Although α for the neighborhood social ties scale is smaller than might be desired, the items used to construct the scale are the best measures available in the PHDCN. In separate analyses, not shown here, including both the neighborhood mean level of number of in-laws and friends separately (the two items that comprise the current scale) led to similar results (available from the author). More on the effect of neighborhood social ties is discussed in the following chapters.

on behalf of the neighborhood if they witnessed children 1) skipping school, 2) vandalizing someone else's property, 3) disrespecting an adult, or 4) fighting in an open area. Respondents were given the following response options based on a 5-item Likert-type scale: very likely, likely, neither likely nor unlikely, unlikely, or very unlikely. The individual-level mean for neighborhood informal social control was 3.40, indicating that the average respondent thought that his or her neighbors were at least somewhat likely to exercise informal social control efforts ($\alpha = 0.82$).

Six items from the PHDCN measure *neighborhood social cohesion*. For these items, respondents were asked how much they agreed or disagreed with statements regarding 1) how closely-knit their neighborhood was, 2) whether neighbors were willing to help each other, 3) whether neighbors did not get along well (reverse-coded), 4) whether people tended to go their own way (reverse-coded), 5) whether they did not shared similar values with their neighbors (reverse-coded), and 6) whether their neighbors could be trusted. Respondents were given the following response options, again based on a 5-item Likert-type scale: strongly agree, agree, neither agree nor disagree, disagree, or strongly disagree. The individual-level mean for neighborhood social cohesion was 2.75, indicating that the average respondent only very slightly agreed that neighbors got along well and shared similar values ($\alpha = 0.75$).

At the neighborhood-level, the two scales used to create the collective efficacy scale (neighborhood informal social control and social cohesion) were highly correlated at 0.78 ($p < 0.001$). The neighborhood-level α for the two scales was 0.85. Following Sampson and colleagues (1999) lead, the two scales were combined to measure neighborhood collective efficacy and are therefore used to determine whether or not neighborhood collective efficacy is a strong predictor of police officers' use of excessive force. As discussed in Chapter 4, it is expected that the neighborhood collective efficacy scale should be negatively related to the dependent variable.

Analytic Strategy

Before discussing the methodology of specific multi-level modeling technique that is employed in this research, it is important to first understand how the results presented in the following chapter can be interpreted as explaining variation in police officers' *actual* use of excessive force, rather than variation only in *civilians' perceptions* of the behaviors, which might be biased for the reasons reviewed above. In order draw to any conclusions regarding the influence of concepts from the social disorganization tradition on actual police behavior, any potential variation in the dependent variable that might be explained by factors related to civilian reporting bias must be held constant.

In the preceding section of this chapter, a number of factors that previous research has linked to civilians' perceptions of the police were discussed. Based on that discussion, 12 individual- and neighborhood-level control variables will be included in the following analyses. Through the inclusion of these control variables, it can then be determined how much variation in the dependent variable may be the result of civilian reporting bias. Once that variation is held constant, the true effect of the social disorganization explanatory variables on police use of excessive force can then be observed. If any of those explanatory variables are significantly related to, and explain additional variation in, the dependent variable, then it can safely be concluded that neighborhood social disorganization is related to actual police behavior, and not simply civilians' reports of police behavior.

There is the some potential that this analytic strategy will *over-control* for certain effects, however. For example, although past research has demonstrated that minorities tend to have more negative perceptions of the police (see review above), they may in fact also experience, and *accurately* report, more problems with police officers' use of excessive force. If this is the case, at least some of the variation in the police use of excessive force variable could be attributed to reporting bias, when it truly might be explained by race/ethnicity or some other variable in the models.[48]   While this is a concern, it also

---

[48] Unfortunately, it is beyond the scope of this research to determine whether or not the following analyses over-control for civilian reporting bias. Research is needed that examines if, and potentially how much, civilians' perceptions of

means that if any significant results are observed for the primary explanatory variables of interest, they will have come from a more conservative test (i.e., less is variation to explain from the start). Consequently, if such conservative tests nevertheless reveal significant results, then those results should be considered robust and it can be safely concluded that a relationship between neighborhood social disorganization and police use of excessive force truly exists.

<u>Multi-Level Modeling Techniques</u>

For this research, multi-level analyses of the variables described above are conducted in order to determine if a social disorganization theory of police use of excessive force is empirically viable. Due to the clustered nature of the PHDCN data (discussed in more detail below), multi-level modeling techniques that correct for the violation of the basic ordinary least squares (OLS) assumption of independence of observations are required.

Traditional OLS regression assumes that the error terms amongst the cases being analyzed are not dependent upon other observed or unobserved factors. In the case of multi-level data, such as in the PHDCN, this assumption is violated. Because respondents who are nested (or clustered) within a neighborhood are more likely to be similar to each other than they are similar to respondents nested within other neighborhoods, the errors of cases within any given neighborhood may not be independent from each other. This dependence can then result in estimates of standard errors that are too small and, subsequently, inaccurate significance tests. To correct for the violation of the independence of errors, the hierarchical linear modeling techniques (HLM) developed by Raudenbush and Bryk (2002) are therefore employed. HLM allows researchers to account for the nesting

---

the police actually bias their reporting of police behavior. While some research has shown that individuals' who are not satisfied with the police are more likely to report police misconduct (see Weitzer 1999, 2002; Weitzer and Tuch 2004), no research has examined whether or not those individuals are more likely to *inaccurately* report police behavior because of their biases.

effect by creating different equations and error terms for each level of data (i.e., one for respondents and one for neighborhoods).

By creating multiple equations and error terms for analysis, any similarity amongst respondents that might be due to unobserved neighborhood-level differences is accounted for in the individual-level error term. In this way, the individual-level error terms then become independent from one another, and in so doing correct for the OLS assumption of independence. With the violation accounted for, HLM then allows researchers to simply conduct basic OLS regression analyses. And, as a result of conducting analyses at multiple levels, the estimates obtained from HLM are more accurate than those that might be obtained using traditional OLS techniques. It should not be misunderstood, however, that HLM techniques will produce radically different results than standard OLS analyses of the same data. Rather, it is very likely that both OLS and HLM regression techniques would produce *generally* similar results (i.e., the same relationships between independent and dependent variables should be observed). However, because HLM provides larger standard errors and subsequently more accurate significance tests, what may have been a statistically significant effect in a standard OLS regression analysis may no longer be significant in an HLM regression analysis.

In addition to producing more accurate estimates, HLM also allows researchers to differentiate individual-level compositional effects from neighborhood-level contextual effects. As mentioned above, because HLM creates separate equations (with separate error terms) for each level of data, any effects that may be due to the composition of the individuals living in a neighborhood (i.e., within-group differences) versus the general context of a neighborhood (i.e. between-group differences) can be fleshed out and identified. In other words, HLM allows researchers to determine exactly how aggregate-level explanatory variables (social disorganization measures, in the case of this research) influence their dependent variables (police use of excessive force for this study), while still accounting for the individual-level differences among respondents living in different neighborhoods.

In terms of interpreting the neighborhood- and individual-level estimates obtained by HLM, one of the most important factors that must be considered is how the individual-level variables are centered. For each of the models discussed below, all of the independent-level civilian reporting bias control variables are grand-mean centered. Although centering affects how researchers should interpret their results, it does not affect model fit, predicted values, or residuals (Raudenbush and Bryk 2002). While group-mean centering centers the variables around each neighborhood's mean level of those variables, grand-mean centering centers the variables around the entire sample's mean value of each variable. Thus, where group-mean centering eliminates all between-neighborhood differences in the individual-level control variables, through the use of grand-mean centering, estimates of the neighborhood-level explanatory variables can be interpreted as changes in the mean levels of police use of excessive force across neighborhoods, net of the individual-level differences among respondents in each neighborhood (i.e., the compositional effects).[49]

HLM also allows me to include random error terms for each variable included in the following models. By adding in, or leaving out, random error terms, researchers can control whether or not the effect of any given variable is allowed to vary across higher levels of aggregation (Raudenbush and Bryk 2002). In other words, for this two-level analysis (individual- and neighborhood-levels), the effect of any of the individual-level control variables can be allowed to vary across neighborhoods. However, because there is no theoretical reason to expect that the effect of the individual-level controls (e.g., race, ethnicity, age, gender) should vary from one neighborhood to the next, no random error terms are included at the individual-level in this study.

The only random error term that is included in any of the models presented below is set on the neighborhood-level intercept. By doing

---

[49] In separate analyses (not shown here, available from the author), the neighborhood-level means of each individual-level reporting bias control variable were included in analyses to control for neighborhood compositional effects. Those analyses showed that there were no significant neighborhood-level compositional effects, and the exclusion of those additional controls did not drastically alter the magnitude of the estimates for any of the primary explanatory variables of interest (the five variables measuring concepts from the social disorganization tradition). As a result, the neighborhood-level means of the individual-level reporting bias controls were excluded from the final analyses discussed here (available from the author).

so, the effects of each of the individual-level control variables is set as being fixed *within* each neighborhood, but, at the same time, allows each neighborhood's intercept, or constant, to vary (i.e., vary *between* neighborhoods). The intercept estimates of the models presented in the following sub-section should therefore be interpreted as the differences in the mean levels of police use of excessive force across each neighborhood in Chicago.

All together, through the use of HLM techniques and the inclusion of individual level control variables, this research improves on the small existing body of research that examines the effects of aggregate-level contextual factors on police use of force. None of the studies reviewed in Chapter 4 (Kane 2002; Lawton 2007; Terrill and Reisig 2003) which utilized multi-level modeling techniques attempted to separately specify and analyze both individual- and neighborhood-level effects to the extent done here. Moreover, because none of those studies defined neighborhoods as precisely as they are defined here, or included as many social disorganization measures as are included here, the results obtained from the analyses that follow will be the first true test of a social disorganization theory of police use of force.

Finally, the use of HLM techniques affords one other important contribution to study the police use of force. As reviewed earlier in this chapter, civilian reporting bias has the potential to invalidate any measures of police use of force obtained via civilian surveys. However, by incorporating both individual- and neighborhood-level control measures into the analysis of civilian survey data, any variation in respondents' reports of police behaviors that might be attributable to either positive or negative perceptions of the police in general can be held constant. Thus, in addition to fully testing a social disorganization theory of police use of force and further demonstrating the full utility of multi-level modeling techniques for the study of police officers' behaviors at the *true* neighborhood-level, this research also provides police use of force researchers with a new and better way to statistically account for reporting bias whenever they use surveys of civilians to study police behavior.

Models for Analysis[50]

The first three models presented below test Hypotheses 1a – 1c, Hypothesis 2a, and Hypothesis 3a (for detailed discussions of each hypothesis, see Chapter 4) and are intended to examine the relationship between each of the three concepts from the social disorganization tradition (neighborhood structural disadvantage, social ties, and collective efficacy) and police officers' use of excessive force. Although these models do not include any of the individual- or neighborhood-level civilian reporting bias controls, it is important to determine whether any relationships among the variables exist in the first place. If they do not, it would then be unnecessary to incorporate any control variables.

Models 1 through 3 below therefore test whether or not each of the three concepts of primary interest from the social disorganization tradition (neighborhood structural disadvantage, social ties, and collective efficacy) can independently predict variation in neighborhood mean levels of police officers' use of excessive force, *without controlling for any other factors* (i.e., any competing social disorganization variables or civilian reporting bias controls). The individual- and neighborhood-level equations for the first three models can therefore be depicted as:

Model 1 – Structural Disadvantage

$$Y_{ij} = \beta_{0j} + r,$$

$$\beta_{0j} = \gamma_{00} + \gamma_{01} \text{ Concentrated Disadvantage}$$
$$+ \gamma_{02} \text{ Concentrated Immigration}$$
$$+ \gamma_{03} \text{ Residential Instability} + u_0$$

---

[50] For each of the models described in this sub-section, let Y_{ij} represent the outcome of interest, police use of excessive force, β_{0j} represent the individual-level intercept, $\beta_1 ... \beta_n$ represent individual-level control variables, r represent the individual-level error term, γ_{00} represent the neighborhood-level intercept, $\gamma_{01} ... \gamma_{0n}$ represent the neighborhood-level explanatory variables of interest, and u_0 represent the neighborhood-level error term.

Model 2 – Systemic Model

$$Y_{ij} = \beta_{0j} + r,$$

$$\beta_{0j} = \gamma_{00} + \gamma_{01 \ Social \ Ties} + u_0$$

Model 3 – Collective Efficacy

$$Y_{ij} = \beta_{0j} + r,$$

$$\beta_{0j} = \gamma_{00} + \gamma_{01 \ Collective \ Efficacy} + u_0$$

If Models 1 – 3 reveal that neighborhood structural factors are related to police use of excessive force, Hypotheses 1a – 1c will be supported and will be preliminary evidence that neighborhood social disorganization may be a viable explanation for police use of excessive force. However, potential measurement error in civilians' reports of police use of excessive force necessitates that any variation potentially due to civilian reporting bias be held constant before any definitive conclusions can be drawn. Therefore the fourth model tested in this study includes the 12 civilian reporting bias control variables described earlier and can be depicted using the following individual- and neighborhood-level equations:

Model 4 – Civilian Reporting Bias Controls

$$
\begin{aligned}
Y_{ij} = \beta_{0j} &+ \beta_1 \ _{Legal \ Cynicism} + \beta_2 \ _{Crime \ Victimization} \\
&+ \beta_3 \ _{Male} + \beta_4 \ _{SES} + \beta_5 \ _{Married} \\
&+ \beta_6 \ _{Number \ of \ Moves \ Past \ 5 \ Years} + \beta_7 \ _{Age \ /10} \\
&+ \beta_8 \ _{Black} + \beta_9 \ _{Hispanic} + \beta_{10} \ _{Asian} \\
&+ \beta_{11} \ _{Other \ Race} + r,
\end{aligned}
$$

$$\beta_{0j} = \gamma_{00} + \gamma_{01 \ NH \ Crime} + u_0$$

If Model 4 does not predict all of the variation in the police use of excessive force, it should be safe to conclude that any remaining unexplained variation represents variation in police officers' *actual* use of excessive force.[51]   Accordingly, the next three models again test Hypotheses 1a – 1c, Hypothesis 2a, and Hypothesis 3a, but this time assess each of the three social disorganization concepts' capacity to explain actual police behavior, net of the controls for civilian reporting bias.   Models 5 through 7 can be depicted using the following individual- and neighborhood-level equations:

Model 5 – Structural Disadvantage (Plus Controls)

$$Y_{ij} = \beta_{0j} + \beta_{1\,Legal\,Cynicism} + \beta_{2\,Crime\,Victimization}$$
$$+ \beta_{3\,Male} + \beta_{4\,SES} + \beta_{5\,Married}$$
$$+ \beta_{6\,Number\,of\,Moves\,Past\,5\,Years} + \beta_{7\,Age/10}$$
$$+ \beta_{8\,Black} + \beta_{9\,Hispanic} + \beta_{10\,Asian}$$
$$+ \beta_{11\,Other\,Race} + r,$$

$$\beta_{0j} = \gamma_{00} + \gamma_{01\,NH\,Crime} + \gamma_{02\,Concentrated\,Disadvantage}$$
$$+ \gamma_{03\,Concentrated\,Immigration}$$
$$+ \gamma_{04\,Residential\,Instability} + u_0$$

Model 6 – Systemic Model (Plus Controls)

$$Y_{ij} = \beta_{0j} + \beta_{1\,Legal\,Cynicism} + \beta_{2\,Crime\,Victimization}$$
$$+ \beta_{3\,Male} + \beta_{4\,SES} + \beta_{5\,Married}$$
$$+ \beta_{6\,Number\,of\,Moves\,Past\,5\,Years} + \beta_{7\,Age/10}$$
$$+ \beta_{8\,Black} + \beta_{9\,Hispanic} + \beta_{10\,Asian}$$
$$+ \beta_{11\,Other\,Race} + r.$$

$$\beta_{0j} = \gamma_{00} + \gamma_{01\,NH\,Crime} + \gamma_{02\,Social\,Ties} + u_0$$

---

[51] Although the inclusion of 12 individual- and neighborhood-level control variables should account for any potential civilian reporting bias, it is possible that there are other important civilian reporting bias factors that should be included in these analyses. Unfortunately, such research is beyond the scope of this book and until any new potential sources of reporting bias can be identified, the control variables utilized in this research should adequately capture the great majority of any bias that might exist.

Model 7 –Collective Efficacy (Plus Controls)

$$Y_{ij} = \beta_{0j} + \beta_1 \, _{Legal\ Cynicism} + \beta_2 \, _{Crime\ Victimization}$$
$$+ \beta_3 \, _{Male} + \beta_4 \, _{SES} + \beta_5 \, _{Married}$$
$$+ \beta_6 \, _{Number\ of\ Moves\ Past\ 5\ Years} + \beta_7 \, _{Age\,/\,10}$$
$$+ \beta_8 \, _{Black} + \beta_9 \, _{Hispanic} + \beta_{10} \, _{Asian}$$
$$+ \beta_{11} \, _{Other\ Race} + r,$$

$$\beta_{0j} = \gamma_{00} + \gamma_{01} \, _{NH\ Crime} + \gamma_{02} \, _{Collective\ Efficacy} + u_0$$

As outlined in Chapter 4, it is expected that neighborhood structural disadvantage should be positively related to police use of excessive force, and that neighborhood social ties and collective efficacy should each be negatively related police use of excessive force. If all three concepts are in fact significant predictors of police officers' use of excessive force, net of the civilian reporting bias controls, there will then be strong support for Hypotheses 1a – 1c, Hypothesis 2a, and Hypothesis 3a. And, if support for those hypotheses can be found, then it should finally be safe to draw more definitive conclusions about the relationship between neighborhood social disorganization and police officers' use of excessive force behaviors.

Based on how the three concepts are theorized to be related to the dependent variable (see Chapter 4), however, it is expected that neighborhood social ties and collective efficacy should mediate the relationship between neighborhood structural disadvantage and police use of excessive force. In order to test for this mediation effect, the neighborhood social ties and collective efficacy variables are independently introduced into Model 5 (Structural Disadvantage [Plus Controls]), thereby assessing the direct and indirect effects of structural disadvantage, net of controls. Subsequently, the eighth and ninth models analyzed in this research test Hypothesis 2b and Hypothesis 3b, and can be depicted using the following individual- and neighborhood-level equations:

Model 8 –Systemic Model Mediation (Plus Controls)

$$Y_{ij} = \beta_{0j} + \beta_1 \text{ Legal Cynicism} + \beta_2 \text{ Crime Victimization}$$
$$+ \beta_3 \text{ Male} + \beta_4 \text{ SES} + \beta_5 \text{ Married}$$
$$+ \beta_6 \text{ Number of Moves Past 5 Years} + \beta_7 \text{ Age}/10$$
$$+ \beta_8 \text{ Black} + \beta_9 \text{ Hispanic} + \beta_{10} \text{ Asian}$$
$$+ \beta_{11} \text{ Other Race} + r,$$

$$\beta_{0j} = \gamma_{00} + \gamma_{01} \text{ NH Crime} + \gamma_{02} \text{ Concentrated Disadvantage}$$
$$+ \gamma_{03} \text{ Concentrated Immigration}$$
$$+ \gamma_{04} \text{ Residential Instability} + \gamma_{05} \text{ Social Ties}$$
$$+ u_0$$

Model 9 –Collective Efficacy Mediation (Plus Controls)

$$Y_{ij} = \beta_{0j} + \beta_1 \text{ Legal Cynicism} + \beta_2 \text{ Crime Victimization}$$
$$+ \beta_3 \text{ Male} + \beta_4 \text{ SES} + \beta_5 \text{ Married}$$
$$+ \beta_6 \text{ Number of Moves Past 5 Years} + \beta_7 \text{ Age}/10$$
$$+ \beta_8 \text{ Black} + \beta_9 \text{ Hispanic} + \beta_{10} \text{ Asian}$$
$$+ \beta_{11} \text{ Other Race} + r,$$

$$\beta_{0j} = \gamma_{00} + \gamma_{01} \text{ NH Crime} + \gamma_{02} \text{ Concentrated Disadvantage}$$
$$+ \gamma_{03} \text{ Concentrated Immigration}$$
$$+ \gamma_{04} \text{ Residential Instability}$$
$$+ \gamma_{05} \text{ Collective Efficacy} + u_0$$

If significant mediating relationships are observed in Models 8 and 9, net of civilian reporting bias controls, there will be strong support for Hypothesis 2b and Hypothesis 3b, indicating that neighborhood social ties and collective efficacy truly are the mechanisms through which neighborhood structural disadvantage leads to increased levels of police use of excessive force.   Such empirical support would lend further credence to the viability of a social disorganization theoretical framework for explaining police behavior as well.

The last model analyzed in this research test Hypothesis 4 and should determine which of the more recent modifications to Shaw & McKay's original social disorganization theory – the systemic model or the collective efficacy framework – is the more robust explanation of police officers' use of excessive force. The tenth and final model analyzed here therefore includes all three of the major concepts from the social disorganization tradition together with the civilian reporting bias controls, and can be depicted using the following individual- and neighborhood-level equations:

Model 10 – Full Social Disorganization (Plus Controls)

$$V_{ij} = \beta_{0j} + \beta_{1 \, Legal \, Cynicism} + \beta_{2 \, Crime \, Victimization}$$
$$+ \beta_{3 \, Male} + \beta_{4 \, SES} + \beta_{5 \, Married}$$
$$+ \beta_{6 \, Number \, of \, Moves \, Past \, 5 \, Years} + \beta_{7 \, Age} / 10$$
$$+ \beta_{8 \, Black} + \beta_{9 \, Hispanic} + \beta_{10 \, Asian}$$
$$+ \beta_{11 \, Other \, Race} + r,$$

$$\beta_{0j} = \gamma_{00} + \gamma_{01 \, NH \, Crime} + \gamma_{02 \, Concentrated \, Disadvantage}$$
$$+ \gamma_{03 \, Concentrated \, Immigration}$$
$$+ \gamma_{04 \, Residential \, Instability} + \gamma_{05 \, Soical \, Ties}$$
$$+ \gamma_{06 \, Collective \, Efficacy} + u_0$$

Based on the recent empirical tests of the systemic model and collective efficacy framework, it is expected that neighborhood collective efficacy will be best predictor of police officers' use of excessive force, net of neighborhood structural disadvantage, social ties, and the civilian reporting bias controls. Should outcome be observed, there will then be strong support for Hypothesis 4 and it will finally be safe to conclude not only that the social disorganization tradition in general, but that the collective efficacy framework in particular, constitutes an empirically-vetted new theoretical explanation of police officers' use of excessive force behaviors. Moreover, it may quite possibly serve as a valuable new approach for studying police behaviors more broadly as well.

CHAPTER 6

The Doubly-Victimized Residents of Disorganized Neighborhoods

This chapter presents and discusses the results of the analyses described in Chapter 5. As the discussion that follows will illustrate in more detail, neighborhood social disorganization was found to strongly predict police officers' use of excessive force, providing compelling evidence for a social disorganization theory of police behavior. As a result, however, the results presented herein also lend credibility the unfortunate possibility first discussed in Chapter 4 that the residents of socially disorganized neighborhoods truly become doubly-victimized – both by the criminals who offend in their neighborhoods and by the police officers who are supposed to protect them, leaving them with nowhere else to turn. Before jumping into the specific results that generated this regrettable conclusion, it is useful to first review each of the analyses that led up to it.

Descriptive Results

Table 6.1 below presents the descriptive statistics for all of the variables included in this research, including the dependent variable (police use of excessive force), the primary explanatory variables of interest (neighborhood structural disadvantage, social ties, and collective efficacy), and each of the individual- and neighborhood-level controls for civilian reporting bias. Beginning with the dependent variable, variation was observed at the individual-level. At this level, the dependent variable ranged from a minimum of 1 to a maximum of 3, with a standard deviation of 0.58.[52] The mean level of police

---

[52] As discussed in Chapter 5, although the dependent variable, police officers' use of excessive force, is measured at the individual-level, for the purposes of the analyses conducted in this research, HLM assesses the effect of each of the explanatory and control variables on changes in the neighborhood mean levels of police use of excessive force (i.e., between-neighborhood effects). More on the neighborhood-level variation in the dependent variable is discussed below.

Table 6.1. Descriptive Statistics

Neighborhood-Level Variables (n_j = 342)	Mean	Std. Dev.	Min.	Max.
Concentrated Disadvantage	0.00	0.99	-1.65	3.81
Concentrated Immigration	0.00	0.97	-1.63	3.07
Residential Instability	0.00	0.98	-2.33	2.18
Social Ties	2.57	0.37	1.59	3.91
Collective Efficacy	3.89	0.26	3.17	4.73
Crime Rate	3.14	0.96	1.30	5.10

Individual-Level Variables (n_i = 8765)	Mean	Std. Dev.	Min.	Max.
Police Use of Excessive Force	1.25	0.58	1	3
White	0.27	0.42	0	1
Black	0.40	0.49	0	1
Hispanic	0.26	0.44	0	1
Asian	0.03	0.16	0	1
Other Race	0.05	0.22	0	1
Age/10	4.27	1.60	1.8	10
Male	0.41	0.49	0	1
Socio-Economic Status	0.00	1.24	-4.08	4.33
Married	0.35	0.48	0	1
Number of Moves Past 5 Years	0.92	1.20	0	5
Legal Cynicism	2.35	0.66	1	5
Past Victimization	0.87	1.01	0	4

officers' use of excessive force was 1.25, indicating that the average respondent thought that use of excessive force by the police in his or her neighborhoods was not much of a problem.

Turning to the neighborhood-level explanatory variables of primary interest in this research (measuring neighborhood social disorganization), there was considerable variation across Chicago neighborhoods. First, regarding the three measures of neighborhood structural disadvantage, neighborhood concentrated disadvantage had a mean of 0 and ranged from a low of -1.65 to a high of 3.81, with a standard deviation of 0.99. Neighborhood concentrated immigration also had a mean of 0 and ranged from -1.63 to 3.07, with a standard deviation of 0.97. Finally, neighborhood residential instability had a mean of 0 as well, and ranged from a minimum of -2.33 to a maximum of 2.18, with a standard deviation of 0.98. Next, neighborhood social ties (measuring the systemic model), had a mean of 2.57, indicating that the average respondent had one to five close relationships with others in their neighborhood. The neighborhood social ties measure ranged from a low 1.59 to a high of 3.91, with a standard deviation of 0.37. Finally, neighborhood collective efficacy had a mean of 3.89, indicating that the average respondent thought that his or her neighbors shared some similar values and goals and were at least somewhat willing to intervene on the behalf of the neighborhood. The neighborhood collective efficacy variable ranged from a minimum of 3.17 to 4.73, with a standard deviation of 0.26.

There was also a good amount of variation in the individual-level civilian reporting bias control variables, as well as the single neighborhood-level measure of crime rates. The neighborhood crime rate variable (homicides) had a mean of 3.14 and ranged from a minimum of 1.30 to a maximum of 5.10, with a standard deviation of 0.96. At the individual-level, 27% of the respondents were white, 40% were black, 26% were Hispanic, 3% were Asian, and 5% identified themselves as being of some other race. Additionally, 41% of the respondents were male and 35% were married. The mean socio-economic status for respondents was 0 and ranged from -4.08 to 4.33, with a standard deviation of 1.24. The average respondent was approximately 43 years of age, with a range from 18 to 100 years old and a standard deviation of 16 years. On average, respondents moved less than once in the past five years, while the total number of moves ranged from 0 to 5, with a standard deviation of 1.20. The average respondent also had lower levels of legal cynicism (mean of 2.35), with reports ranging from a low of 1 to a high of 5 and a standard deviation of 0.66. Finally, the average respondent had not been the victim of any crimes, although victimization ranged from a minimum of 0 experiences to a maximum of 4 previous experiences, with a standard deviation of 1.01.

Before describing the results of the more sophisticated analyses, however, it is first important to establish that there is variation in the dependent variable that can be explained. Unlike other multi-level analyses using HLM, the ordinal regressions that are conducted for this research do not report both within- and between-neighborhood variance components (Bryk and Raudenbush 2002). Instead, HLM reports only the between-neighborhood variance component. Fortunately, this is not a problem for the purposes of this research. Because the focus of this research lies only in what influence each of the explanatory and control variables have on the mean level of police officers' use of excessive force across neighborhoods, only the between-neighborhood variance component is necessary.

In order to obtain the between-neighborhood variance component for the dependent variable, an analysis of only that variable, police use of excessive force, was conducted with no covariates included in the model. The results of this null model revealed that there is indeed significant variation in the mean level of police use of excessive force across neighborhoods. The between-neighborhoods variance component was 0.931 ($p < 0.001$). The sections that follow discuss the amount of between-neighborhood variation which can be attributed to the explanatory and/or control variables included in each model using the following equation: $y = ((0.931 - x)/0.931)*100$, where y represents the percentage of the variation explained by the covariates, 0.931 is the total amount of variation that is available to be explained, and x represents the variance component for each specific model that is tested. The results of the bivariate analyses examining the individual effects of each of the three primary social disorganization concepts on police use of excessive force are presented and discussed first.

Bivariate Results

Table 6.2 below presents the results of the three bivariate tests of Models 1 through 3 (presented in Chapter 5). These bivariate tests are necessary in order to demonstrate that a link between neighborhood social disorganization and police officers' use of force did in fact exist. Had none of the three concepts from the social disorganization tradition – neighborhood structural disadvantage, neighborhood social ties, and neighborhood collective efficacy – been significant predictors of police use of excessive force in stand-alone tests, then none of the following analyses would have been necessary. Fortunately, however, with only a single exception, the primary social disorganization explanatory variables of interest were all significantly related to the police use of excessive force in the expected direction.

Model 1 in Table 6.2 displays the bivariate results for the component effects of neighborhood structural disadvantage (neighborhood concentrated disadvantage, neighborhood concentrated immigration, and residential instability) on police officers' use of excessive force. Although Model 1 was not a true bivariate analysis of the effect of each component measure of neighborhood structural disadvantage on the dependent variable, because the three measures are commonly analyzed together and were intended to collectively measure one concept, the effect of all three variables were analyzed together in a single model (for precedent, see Morenoff et al. 1997; Sampson et al. 1997; Sampson et al. 1999). Subsequently, as Model 1 shows, each of the three component measures of neighborhood structural disadvantage were positively and significantly ($p < 0.001$) related to police officers' use of excessive force. And, of the component measures included in this preliminary analysis, it appears that neighborhood concentrated disadvantage had the strongest effect on police use of excessive force, while neighborhood residential instability had the weakest. More on the substantive meaning of these effects is discussed below.

Perhaps the most surprising result to be found in Model 1 is that when none of the social disorganization explanatory variables or civilian reporting bias control variables were included in the model, neighborhood structural disadvantage explained a remarkable 70% of

Table 6.2. Neighborhood-Level Bivariate Relationships with Police Use of Excessive Force ($n_j = 342$; $n_i = 8765$)

Neighborhood-Level Variables	Model 1			Model 2			Model 3		
	β	Exp (β)	Std. Err.	β	Exp (β)	Std. Err.	β	Exp (β)	Std. Err.
Concentrated Disadvantage	0.78	2.18 ***	(0.05)						
Concentrated Immigration	0.32	1.38 ***	(0.04)						
Residential Instability	0.14	1.15 ***	(0.05)						
Social Ties				-0.15	0.86	(0.16)			
Collective Efficacy							-1.26	0.29 ***	(0.20)
Variance Explained		70%			7%			52%	

Notes: *** p < 0.001; ** p < 0.01; * p < 0.05

the variation in police officers' use of excessive force.[53] Thus, at least in these preliminary analyses, neighborhood structural disadvantage appears to be an important direct predictor of police officers' use of excessive force. The findings of Model 1 therefore provide some initial support for the neighborhood structural disadvantage hypotheses described in Chapter 4 (Hypotheses 1a through 1c).

Model 2 in Table 6.2 displays the results for bivariate effect of neighborhood social ties on police use of excessive force. Neighborhood social ties were not significantly related to the dependent variable, although the effect was in the expected direction.[54] This result was somewhat surprising since previous research on the systemic model had observed a significant, negative effect of neighborhood social ties on crime rates, but not all that surprising too, given that other research had found that those same ties might actually promote crime (Bellair 1997; Browning et al. 2004; Patillo-McCoy 1999; Sampson et al. 1997; Wilson 1996). Nonetheless, in regards to its effect on police officers' use of excessive force, the systemic model does not appear to be a viable explanation. The findings of Model 2 therefore provide

---

[53] Although it may seem surprising that a single concept from the social disorganization tradition explains so much variation in the dependent variable (70%), recall that neighborhood structural disadvantage is comprised of three separate measures, all of which are comprised of a number of other measures (see Chapter 5 for details). Subsequently, the concept of neighborhood structural disadvantage is actually measuring the influence of a large number of factors on police use of excessive force, so it should not be wholly unexpected that such a large amount of variation is accounted for in Model 1. Moreover, once additional covariates are added to the multivariate models discussed later in this chapter, it is likely that the amount of variation explained by neighborhood structural disadvantage will be reduced. The results of all the remaining bivariate models should therefore be viewed judiciously as well.

[54] Although the effect of neighborhood social ties was non-significant, with no covariates in the model, neighborhood social ties did explain 7% of the between-neighborhood variance in police officers' use of excessive force. Furthermore, as with the amount of variation explained by neighborhood structural disadvantage, once other explanatory and control variables are added in the multivariate models, the amount of variance explained by the systemic model will likely be even less.

some preliminary evidence that challenges the neighborhood systemic model hypotheses described in Chapter 4 (Hypotheses 2a and 2c).

Finally, Model 3 in Table 6.2 presents the results of the bivariate test of neighborhood collective efficacy on police officers' use of excessive force. As expected, neighborhood collective efficacy was negatively and significantly ($p < 0.001$) related to the dependent variable. Moreover, this bivariate test revealed that neighborhood collective efficacy had the potential to explain upwards of 52% of the variation in police officers' use of excessive force.[55] Although this bivariate test did not include any covariates, Model 3 nonetheless provides some tentative support for the collective efficacy hypotheses described in Chapter 4 (Hypotheses 3a and 3b).

To briefly summarize, Models 1 through 3 in Table 6.2 provide some initial support for relationships between two of the concepts from the social disorganization tradition and police officers' use of excessive force. With the exception of the effect of neighborhood social ties, there is subsequently good reason to believe that the neighborhood social disorganization tradition, and a collective efficacy framework in particular, may indeed be a viable new theoretical framework for explaining police use of excessive force. However, before more definitive conclusions can be drawn, it must be shown that the concepts from the social disorganization tradition have the capacity to explain variation in police use of excessive force net of controls for civilian reporting bias.

Civilian Reporting Bias Results

Table 6.3 below presents the results of the civilian reporting bias controls analysis (Model 4 from Chapter 5). In order to determine how much of the variation in police officers' use of excessive force might be attributable to factors associated with civilians' perceptions of the police, the 11 of the individual-level control variables and the single neighborhood-level control variable that were discussed in Chapter 5

---

[55] As with each of the previous models in Table 6.2, the amount of variation explained by Model 3 is likely to decrease when the other explanatory and control variables are introduced in later models.

Table 6.3. Ordinal Regression Model Predicting Civilian Reporting Bias

	Model 4		
	β	Exp (β)	Std. Err.
Constant 1	-3.31	0.04 ***	(0.21)
Constant 2	-1.16	0.31 ***	(0.04)
Neighborhood-Level Variables (n_j = 342)			
Crime Rate	0.47	1.60 ***	(0.06)
Individual-Level Variables (n_i = 8765)			
Black	0.69	2.00 ***	(0.13)
Hispanic	0.75	2.12 ***	(0.12)
Asian	0.24	1.27 ***	(0.22)
Other Race	0.11	1.11 *	(0.14)
Age/10	-0.64	0.53 ***	(0.03)
Male	0.17	1.18 ***	(0.06)
Socioeconomic Status	-0.41	0.67 ***	(0.03)
Married	0.04	1.04	(0.06)
Number of Moves Past 5 Years	-0.04	0.96	(0.03)
Legal Cynicism	0.31	1.36 ***	(0.05)
Past Victimization	0.40	1.49 ***	(0.03)
Variance Explained		65%	

Notes: *** $p < 0.001$; ** $p < 0.01$; * $p < 0.05$

were analyzed with none of the social disorganization explanatory variables of primary interest included in the model. Then, if there is any variation left in the dependent variable after accounting for the effects of the civilian reporting bias controls, this remaining amount should represent variation in actual police use of excessive force behaviors, rather than any reporting bias that might be due to civilians' perceptions of the police.[56]

Before discussing the amount of variation that the civilian reporting bias control variables accounted for in police use of excessive force, it is instructive to briefly review some of the relationships that were observed. First, at the neighborhood-level, neighborhood crime (homicide) rates were positively and significantly related to respondents' reports of police officers' using excessive force. Then, at the individual-level, racial/ethnic minority respondents had greater odds of reporting problems with police officers' use of excessive force in comparison to white respondents. Older and higher socioeconomic status respondents had lower odds for reporting problems, while male respondents had greater odds of reporting problems with police use of excessive force. Not surprisingly, respondents who had higher levels of legal cynicism, or who had been criminally victimized in the past also reported more problems with police use of excessive force. Finally, neither marital status nor the number of moves in the past five years for each respondent were significantly related to respondents'

---

[56] As previously discussed in Chapter 5, there is the possibility that this analytic strategy *over*-controls for civilian reporting bias and in doing so eliminates some of the variation in police officers' use of excessive force that may actually be due to other factors. For example, minority respondents might not only make potentially biased reports about police use of force, but they may actually experience more use of excessive force at the hands of the police as well. However, if significant results for the social disorganization concepts are observed in this more conservative test, the results should be considered even more robust than if civilian reporting bias had not been over-controlled. Thus, even though over-controlling for civilian reporting bias is not a major problem for this research, a more nuanced examination of civilians' perceptions of, and the actual experiences with, police use of excessive force might be an interesting avenue for future research.

reports of police use of excessive force.[57]   At both the neighborhood- and individual-levels then, these results are consistent with past research (see Chapter 5).   Nevertheless, because the relationships between the concepts from the social disorganization tradition and police officers' actual use of excessive force are the primary focus of this research, the most important finding from Table 6.3 is that there was still a substantial amount of variation left to be explained even after accounting for the civilian reporting bias controls.

As indicated in Table 6.3, the individual- and neighborhood-level civilian reporting bias control variables combined to account for only 65% of the variation in the dependent variable.   While 65% of the variation may seem like a large percentage of the variation in police officers' use of excessive force, there is still a good amount of variation (35%) that remains unexplained.[58]   Subsequently, if the introduction of any of the social disorganization concepts into this control model explains any additional variation in police officers' use of excessive force, then it is safe to conclude that those concepts are explaining part of that 35% of the variation in the dependent variable *not* attributable to civilian reporting bias.   Thus, for the remainder of the models discussed in this chapter (which include all 12 of the individual- and neighborhood- level civilian reporting bias controls), findings are discussed in terms of how much additional variation in the dependent variable each of the social disorganization concepts can explain *above and beyond* the amount of variation attributable to the civilian reporting

---

[57] In the multivariate analyses discussed below, the effects of the individual- and neighborhood-level civilian reporting bias controls stay largely the same as they are reported here.   That is, with the exception of small changes in effect sizes and the effects of a few variables becoming non-significant in later models, there are no major changes to the civilian reporting bias estimates discussed here.   Consequently, because the concepts from the social disorganization tradition are of primary interest for this research, the estimates of the civilian reporting bias controls will not be discussed to any further extent throughout the remainder of this chapter.

[58] Furthermore, as with all of the previous models in Table 6.2, the amount of variation explained by the civilian reporting bias control variables is likely to decrease when the substantive explanatory variables of interest are introduced in the multivariate models discussed below.

bias controls. Furthermore, as discussed above (and in Chapter 5), once the variation attributable to civilian reporting bias is held constant, any additional variance explained by the explanatory variables of interest (above 65%) is considered to be the amount of variation explained in *actual* levels of police use of excessive force.

Multivariate Results

Table 6.4 below presents the results of the multivariate tests of Models 5 through 10, as they were described in Chapter 5. Beginning with Model 5 of Table 6.4, neighborhood structural disadvantage was positively and significantly related to police officers' use of excessive force, net of the individual- and neighborhood-level civilian reporting bias controls. As expected, each of the three measures of neighborhood structural disadvantage was positively related to the dependent variable, providing more robust support for Hypotheses 1a through 1c. Breaking it down by each component measure, and starting with neighborhood concentrated disadvantage, a one standard deviation unit increase in disadvantage corresponded to a 45% increase in the odds that police use of excessive force would become more of a problem ($p < 0.001$), net of the civilian reporting bias controls. Similarly, for each standard deviation unit increase in neighborhood concentrated immigration and residential instability, the odds that police use of excessive force would become more of a problem increased by 29% and 18% respectively ($p \leq 0.001$ for each effect).

Of the three measures of neighborhood structural disadvantage, it appears that neighborhood concentrated disadvantage (percentage in poverty, on welfare, unemployed, black, and living in female-headed households with kids) was the strongest and most robust predictor of police officers' use of excessive force. As the collective concept of neighborhood structural disadvantage, however, the three component measures account for 11% percent of the variation in actual police use of excessive force behavior (76% - 65% = 11%). Based on these results, Hypotheses 1a through 1c are therefore supported by the data. And, after only one civilian reporting bias control model, there is compelling evidence that the social disorganization tradition might be a viable theoretical framework for studying police officers' use of force.

Table 6.4. Ordinal Regression Models Predicting Police Use of Excessive Force

	Model 5			Model 6			Model 7		
	β	Exp (β)	Std. Err.	β	Exp (β)	Std. Err.	β	Exp (β)	Std. Err.
Constant 1	-2.49	0.08 ***	(0.25)	-3.29	0.04 ***	(0.36)	3.00	20.14 **	(0.98)
Constant 2	-1.17	0.31 ***	(0.04)	-1.16	0.31 ***	(0.04)	-1.17	0.31 ***	(0.04)
Neighborhood-Level Variables (n_j = 342)									
Concentrated Disadvantage	0.37	1.45 ***	(0.08)						
Concentrated Immigration	0.25	1.29 ***	(0.05)						
Residential Instability	0.17	1.18 ***	(0.05)						
Social Ties				-0.01	0.99	(0.11)			
Collective Efficacy							-0.65	0.52 ***	(0.22)
Crime Rate	0.19	1.21 *	(0.08)	0.47	1.60 ***	(0.06)	0.24	1.28 ***	(0.07)
Individual-Level Variables (n_i = 8765)									
Black	0.82	2.26 ***	(0.14)	0.69	2.00 ***	(0.13)	0.70	2.02 ***	(0.11)
Hispanic	0.65	1.91 ***	(0.12)	0.75	2.12 ***	(0.12)	0.71	2.03 ***	(0.11)
Asian	0.23	1.26 ***	(0.22)	0.24	1.27 ***	(0.22)	0.23	1.25 ***	(0.20)
Other Race	0.10	1.10	(0.14)	0.11	1.11 *	(0.14)	0.09	1.10	(0.15)
Age/10	-0.60	0.55 ***	(0.03)	-0.63	0.53 ***	(0.03)	-0.62	0.54 ***	(0.02)
Male	0.18	1.20 ***	(0.06)	0.17	1.19 ***	(0.06)	0.17	1.19 ***	(0.06)
Socioeconomic Status	-0.35	0.71 ***	(0.03)	-0.41	0.66 ***	(0.03)	-0.39	0.68 ***	(0.03)
Married	-0.03	0.97	(0.06)	-0.04	0.96	(0.06)	-0.03	0.97	(0.07)
Number of Moves Past 5 Years	-0.06	0.94	(0.03)	-0.04	0.96	(0.03)	-0.07	0.93	(0.03)
Legal Cynicism	0.30	1.34 ***	(0.05)	0.31	1.36 ***	(0.05)	0.31	1.37 ***	(0.04)
Past Victimization	0.40	1.49 ***	(0.03)	0.40	1.49 ***	(0.03)	0.39	1.48 ***	(0.03)
Variance Explained	76%			65%			71%		

Notes: *** $p < 0.001$; ** $p < 0.01$; * $p < 0.05$

Table 6.4. Ordinal Regression Models Predicting Police Use of Excessive Force (Contd.)

	Model 8			Model 9			Model 10		
	β	Exp (β)	Std. Err.	β	Exp (β)	Std. Err.	β	Exp (β)	Std. Err.
Constant 1	-2.37	0.09 ***	(0.42)	0.50	1.65	(1.05)	0.54	1.72	(1.04)
Constant 2	-1.17	0.31 ***	(0.04)	-1.17	0.31 ***	(0.04)	-1.17	0.31 ***	(0.04)
Neighborhood-Level Variables (n$_j$ = 342)									
Concentrated Disadvantage	0.38	1.46 ***	(0.07)	0.31	1.37 ***	(0.07)	0.30	1.35 ***	(0.08)
Concentrated Immigration	0.25	1.29 ***	(0.05)	0.22	1.25 ***	(0.05)	0.21	1.24 ***	(0.05)
Residential Instability	0.17	1.18 ***	(0.05)	0.11	1.12 *	(0.05)	0.12	1.12 *	(0.05)
Social Ties	-0.03	0.97	(0.13)				0.07	1.07	(0.13)
Collective Efficacy				-0.33	0.72 **	(0.24)	-0.36	0.70 **	(0.26)
Crime Rate	0.19	1.21 ***	(0.08)	0.13	1.14	(0.08)	0.13	1.14	(0.08)
Individual-Level Variables (n$_i$ = 8765)									
Black	0.81	2.25 ***	(0.12)	0.79	2.21 ***	(0.12)	0.80	2.23 ***	(0.12)
Hispanic	0.65	1.91 ***	(0.11)	0.64	1.89 ***	(0.11)	0.64	1.89 ***	(0.11)
Asian	0.23	1.26 ***	(0.20)	0.23	1.26 ***	(0.20)	0.23	1.25 ***	(0.20)
Other Race	0.10	1.10	(0.15)	0.09	1.10	(0.15)	0.09	1.10	(0.15)
Age/10	-0.61	0.55 ***	(0.02)	-0.61	0.55 ***	(0.02)	-0.61	0.55 ***	(0.02)
Male	0.18	1.19 ***	(0.06)	0.18	1.19 ***	(0.06)	0.18	1.19 ***	(0.06)
Socioeconomic Status	-0.34	0.71 ***	(0.03)	-0.34	0.71 ***	(0.03)	-0.34	0.71 ***	(0.03)
Married	-0.03	0.97	(0.07)	-0.03	0.97	(0.07)	-0.03	0.97	(0.07)
Number of Moves Past 5 Years	-0.06	0.94	(0.03)	-0.06	0.94	(0.03)	-0.06	0.94	(0.03)
Legal Cynicism	0.30	1.34 ***	(0.04)	0.30	1.34 ***	(0.04)	0.30	1.34 ***	(0.04)
Past Victimization	0.40	1.49 ***	(0.03)	0.40	1.49 ***	(0.03)	0.40	1.49 ***	(0.03)
Variance Explained		76%			78%			78%	

Notes: *** p < 0.001; ** p < 0.01; * p < 0.05

Model 6 in Table 6.4 shows the results for the systemic model, net of the individual- and neighborhood-level civilian reporting bias controls. Although no significant relationship between neighborhood social ties and police officers' use of excessive force were observed in Model 2 above, Model 6 helps determine whether a suppression effect might exist as a result of the civilian reporting bias controls being included in the analysis. Based on the estimated shown in Model 6, however, no such suppression effect is evident. As was found in the no-control model (Model 2 above), neighborhood social ties were not significantly related to police officers' use of force, net of the civilian reporting bias controls, although they did predict change in the dependent variable in the expected direction once again. Not surprisingly, the addition of the neighborhood social ties measure did not explain any variation in actual police use of excessive force (65% - 65% = 0%), as compared to the controls-only model (Model 4). Based on the estimates presented in Model 6, Hypotheses 2a is therefore not supported by the data. Subsequently, even though this finding does not preclude the possibility of a social disorganization theory of police use of force behavior, it does make the viability of a neighborhood systemic model explanation very unlikely.

In comparison to the findings for the systemic model (Model 6), the viability of a collective efficacy explanation for police officers' use of excessive force receives much more support. As shown in Model 7 of Table 6.4, net of the individual- and neighborhood-level civilian reporting bias controls, neighborhood collective efficacy was strongly related to police officers' use of excessive force. It was hypothesized in Chapter 4 that collective efficacy would be negatively related to the dependent variable (Hypotheses 3a and 3b), and Model 7 bears this out. In more specific terms, a one standard deviation unit increase in a neighborhood's level of collective efficacy corresponded to a 48% decrease in the odds that police officers' use of excessive force would become more of a problem ($p < 0.001$).

Of the results discussed thus far, the effect of neighborhood collective efficacy has been the largest in magnitude. However, compared to Model 5 above, the introduction of collective efficacy into the base civilian reporting bias model (Model 4) does not explain as much variation in the actual police use of force as did Model 5 (neighborhood structural disadvantage). That is, neighborhood collective efficacy only explained 6% of the variation in actual police use of excessive force (71% - 65% = 6%), whereas neighborhood structural disadvantage explained 11%. Nonetheless, Hypothesis 3a was supported by the data. Subsequently, Model 7 provides not only more compelling evidence for a social disorganization theory of police use of excessive force more generally, it provides strong evidence for a more specific neighborhood collective efficacy framework as well.

To briefly summarize the findings of Models 5 through 7, neighborhood structural disadvantage and neighborhood collective efficacy were both strongly and significantly related to police officers' use of excessive force in the expected directions. The effect of neighborhood social ties, however, was not significant. So, while Model 5 and Model 7 provide compelling evidence that at least two of the concepts from the social disorganization tradition are related to police use of force behavior, in order to truly test the viability of social disorganization explanation, the data should also reveal that neighborhood social ties and neighborhood collective efficacy mediate the neighborhood structural disadvantage-police use of excessive force relationship. Models 8 and 9 therefore present the results of the two social disorganization mediation analyses.

Model 8 in Table 6.4 displays the results of the neighborhood systemic mediation model, net of the civilian reporting bias controls, and tests Hypothesis 2b from Chapter 4. As is evident from the results, however, no support was found for this hypothesis. Once again, neighborhood social ties were not significantly related to police officers' use of excessive force. Interestingly, however, in comparison to Model 5, the magnitude of the neighborhood concentrated disadvantage effect in Model 8 was approximately 2% greater after the neighborhood social ties measure was added into the analysis ($p < 0.001$). This was the only noteworthy change between Models 5 and 8, though. The introduction of the neighborhood social ties variable again had no effect on the amount of variance explained. Just as was observed in Model 5, Model 8 explained only 11% of the variation in police use of excessive force (76% - 65% = 11%). Based on Model 8 then, the data offered no new evidence that the amount of social ties that residents shared with each other was an important factor in predicting police officers' use of force. Hypothesis 2a and 2b were therefore not supported by the data and a neighborhood systemic model explanation of police use of excessive force does not appear viable.

Unlike the results for Model 8, Model 9 in Table 6.4 reveals that neighborhood collective efficacy was indeed a viable explanation for police officers' use of excessive force. Model 9 specifically tested Hypothesis 3b from Chapter 4, and although a full mediation effect was not observed, the results show that the introduction of the neighborhood collective efficacy variable does at least partially mediate the relationship between neighborhood structural disadvantage and police officers' use of excessive force. Specifically, in comparison to Model 5, the introduction of the neighborhood collective efficacy variable reduced the magnitude of the effect of neighborhood concentrated disadvantage by 19% (p < 0.001), the effect of neighborhood concentrated immigration by 14% (p < 0.001), and the effect of neighborhood residential instability by 35% (and also reduced its level of significance to p < 0.05).

The effect of neighborhood collective efficacy also was reduced, however. In comparison to Model 7, the magnitude of the effect of neighborhood collective efficacy in Model 9 was reduced by approximately 49%.[59] Nonetheless, among the neighborhood-level explanatory variables of interest in Model 9, the collective efficacy variable still had one of the strongest impacts on the dependent variable. That is, net of all the other covariates, a one standard deviation unit increase in neighborhood collective efficacy reduced the odds of having more problems with police officers' use of excessive force by 28% (the level of significance is reduced to p < 0.01 as well). In comparison, increases in neighborhood concentrated disadvantage corresponded to a 37% increase in the odds that police officers' use of excessive force is a problem, while increases in neighborhood concentrated immigration corresponded to a 25% increase in the odds,

---

[59] Although the effect of neighborhood collective efficacy was reduced to a greater extent than the effects of any of the component measures of neighborhood structural disadvantage, because the social disorganization tradition predicts that collective efficacy should be a result of structural disadvantage (see Morenoff et al. 2001; Sampson et al. 1999; Sampson et al. 1997), and therefore temporally subsequent to it, the estimates presented in Model 9 are interpreted as being supportive of a collective efficacy mediation effect.

and increases in neighborhood residential instability corresponded to only a 12% increase in the odds. Thus, even though the magnitude of their effects were reduced by introducing the neighborhood collective efficacy variable into the model, the three component measures of neighborhood structural still had significant, direct effects on police officers' use of excessive force.

The combined effects of neighborhood structural disadvantage and neighborhood collective efficacy also accounted for a total of 13% of the variation in actual police use of excessive force (78% - 65% = 13%). Compared to the structural-disadvantage-only model (Model 5), Model 9 explained an additional 2% of the variation in the dependent variable. While the inclusion of neighborhood collective efficacy does not explain a large amount of the variation in police officers' use of excessive force above and beyond the structural-disadvantage-only model, combined they do account for well over a third of the total variation in actual police use of excessive force (i.e., the remaining variance once civilian reporting bias is held constant).

So, even though the results of Model 9 show that neighborhood collective efficacy does not completely mediate the relationship between neighborhood structural disadvantage and police use of excessive force, and it only accounts for a small additional percentage of the explained variance, it does partially mediate the relationship. Moreover, of all the social disorganization concepts examined, it had one of the greatest impacts on police use of excessive force. Hypothesis 3b is therefore partially supported by the data, indicating that the social disorganization tradition more generally, and a collective efficacy explanation in particular, may in fact be strong theoretical frameworks for explaining police officers' use of excessive force.

The final model analyzed in this book combined all three of the concepts from the social disorganization tradition – neighborhood structural disadvantage, social ties, and collective efficacy – into a single analysis that tested Hypothesis 4 and the second larger research question (see Chapter 4) regarding the importance of neighborhood collective efficacy within the social disorganization tradition. Briefly, it was questioned whether or not collective efficacy was the most important factor in predicting police officers' use of excessive force in comparison to the two other concepts from the social disorganization tradition. Then, based on the arguments laid out in Chapter 4, it was specifically hypothesized that, net of all the other social disorganization tradition concepts *and* all of the individual- and neighborhood-level civilian reporting bias controls, neighborhood collective efficacy would be the best predictor of police officers' use of excessive force. Should Hypothesis 4 be supported by the data, there will then be very compelling evidence that neighborhood collective efficacy is the driving force behind a social disorganization tradition explanation for police officers' use of excessive force behaviors.

Model 10 in Table 6.4 displays the results of the empirical test of Hypothesis 4. As shown in Model 10, net of all the other covariates, neighborhood collective efficacy had one of the strongest influences on the odds that police use of excessive force would become a bigger problem in a neighborhood, even relative to all the other measures from the social disorganization tradition. Somewhat surprisingly, however, it was actually neighborhood concentrated disadvantage that had the greatest impact on police officers' use of excessive force. Specifically, a one standard deviation increase in neighborhood concentrated disadvantage corresponded to a 35% increase in the odds that police use of excessive force would become more of a problem, compared to a one standard deviation increase in neighborhood collective efficacy, which corresponded to only a 30% decrease in the odds.

One possible explanation for the above discrepancy in effect sizes is the large number of neighborhood structural characteristics that were captured by the concentrated disadvantage measure (i.e., both racial and economic compositional characteristics, see Chapter 5 for details). Because the neighborhood concentrated disadvantage variable actually measured the greatest number of neighborhood structural characteristics of all the variables utilized for this research, it should not be too surprising that it had such a large impact on police officers' use of excessive force. Nevertheless, neighborhood collective efficacy still had the second largest influence on police use of excessive force, providing at least partial support for Hypothesis 4.

In addition to the interesting findings described above, the inclusion of the neighborhood social ties variable between Models 9 and 10 appeared to result in a suppression effect. In other words, a one unit increase in neighborhood collective efficacy now corresponded with a 2% greater decrease in the odds that police officers' use of excessive force would become more of a problem in a neighborhood (p < 0.01). Substantively, what all these findings mean is simply that neighborhoods with high levels of collective efficacy (i.e., high social cohesion and informal social control), should have much lower odds of experiencing problems with police officers' use of excessive force than neighborhoods with lower levels of collective efficacy, net of not only civilian reporting bias controls, but also net of neighborhood structural disadvantage and neighborhood social ties.

To help illustrate the effect of neighborhood collective efficacy, Figure 6.1 (below) graphically depicts the predicted probabilities of low, average, and high collective efficacy neighborhoods experiencing more problems with police officers' use of excessive force (i.e., moving up one level on the scale of the dependent variable), holding all of the other covariates in the model constant.[60] As the figure below shows, neighborhoods with the lowest level of collective efficacy were much more likely to experience problems with police officers' use of force (27.9%) than were neighborhoods with the highest level of collective efficacy (5.4%). In other words, neighborhoods with low social cohesion and few residents willing to engage in informal social control efforts have a 27.9% chance of police use of excessive force becoming more of a problem, while their counterpart neighborhoods with high collective efficacy only have a 5.4% chance of the same thing occurring. Based on this final model, which included all of the other social disorganization tradition concepts and all of the civilian reporting bias controls, it therefore appears that the neighborhood collective

---

[60] To calculate the predicted probabilities presented in Figures 6.1 and 6.2 (below), an equation using the estimates obtained from Model 10 was created. The minimum, mean, and maximum values for neighborhood collective efficacy and neighborhood structural disadvantage were then entered into the equation. The values of all the other neighborhood-level variables (including neighborhood crime rate) that were not of primary interest for each specific figure were held constant at their neighborhood-level means. Additionally, because all of the individual-level civilian reporting bias control variables were grand-mean centered, their total effect at the neighborhood level was equal to zero, so the individual-level estimates were not included in the equation.

efficacy framework is both a very strong, and very robust, explanation of police officers' use of excessive force behaviors.

Figure 6.1. Neighborhood Collective Efficacy and the Predicted Probability of Police Use of Excessive Force becoming More of a Problem

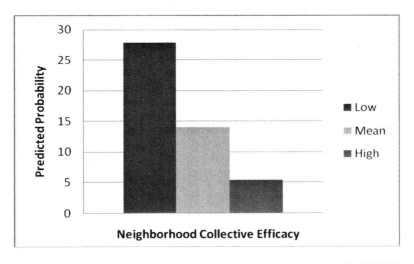

While the results of Model 10 revealed that there was only a small change in the magnitude of the effect size for neighborhood collective efficacy, there were a few other small differences between the final model and some of the earlier models that had been tested. First, the biggest change of note between Model 10 and several of the earlier models was that the effect of neighborhood social ties switched from having a negative relationship with police officers' use of excessive force to having a positive relationship. Because the estimated effect of neighborhood social ties on police use of excessive force was still non-significant, however, it is difficult to determine what this change in the direction of the effect truly means.[61]

---

[61] Because the effect of neighborhood social ties was not statistically significant, the predicted probabilities of neighborhoods with high, mean, and

The only other small differences between the Model 10 and some of the earlier models are all related to the change in the effect sizes of the three measures of neighborhood structural disadvantage. Compared to Model 9 (the neighborhood collective efficacy mediation model), the magnitude of the effects for neighborhood concentrated disadvantage and neighborhood concentrated immigration were reduced by less than 1% each, although both remained significant ($p < 0.001$), when the measure of neighborhood social ties is introduced into the analysis. The effect size and significance of neighborhood residential instability was unchanged between Models 9 and 10.   Thus, it appears that neighborhood structural disadvantage has a direct effect on police use of excessive force, net of both neighborhood social ties and neighborhood collective efficacy.   Substantively, this means neighborhoods with high levels of disadvantage, immigration, and residential instability have greater odds of experiencing problems with police use of excessive force than do neighborhoods with lower levels. Furthermore, it also means that the effect of neighborhood concentrated disadvantage is not fully mediated by neighborhood social ties or levels of collective efficacy as many social disorganization theorists had predicted (e.g., Morenoff et al. 2001; Sampson et al. 1999; Sampson et al. 1997).

To illustrate the direct effect of neighborhood structural disadvantage, net of all other variables included in this analysis, Figure 6.2 (below) graphically depicts the predicted probabilities of having problems with police use of excessive force in neighborhoods with low, mean, and high levels of structural disadvantage. As the figure shows, the combined effects of all three measures of neighborhood structural disadvantage have a very strong influence on the probability of police use of excessive force being a problem. Specifically, neighborhoods with the lowest levels of structural disadvantage (concentrated disadvantage, concentrated immigration, and residential instability) have only a 6.4% chance of having problems, while neighborhoods with the greatest amount of structural disadvantage have a staggering 32.3% chance of experiencing problems with police use of excessive

---

low levels of the variable having problems with police use of excessive force are not presented here (available from the author).

force. Consequently, it appears that the combined effect of all three neighborhood structural disadvantage measures had the strongest effect on the likelihood that a neighborhood would experience problems with police officers' use of excessive force.

Figure 6.2. Neighborhood Structural Disadvantage and the Predicted Probability of Police Use of Excessive Force becoming More of a Problem

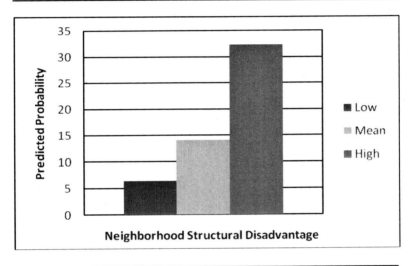

Together with the results of Model 10, Figures 6.1 and 6.2 suggest that both neighborhood structural disadvantage and collective efficacy are strong, robust predictors of police officers' use of excessive force behaviors, and that the influence of neighborhood social ties is negligible. On its own, neighborhood collective efficacy had one of the largest influences on the odds that police officers' use of excessive force would become more of a problem in a neighborhood, but the singular effect of neighborhood concentrated disadvantage and the combined effects of all three components of neighborhood structural disadvantage as a whole were the strongest predictors that a neighborhood might experience more problems with police officers'

use of excessive force. More simply put, when all the concepts from the social disorganization tradition were included in the same model simultaneously, the data only partially supported Hypothesis 4, such that neighborhood collective efficacy was *one of the strongest predictors* of police officers' use of excessive force, but only when compared to two of the three component measures of neighborhood structural disadvantage and the single measure of neighborhood social ties.

Finally, in addition to partially supporting Hypothesis 4, the combined effects of all of the concepts from the social disorganization tradition explained 13% of the variation in actual police use of excessive force (78% - 65% = 13%). In comparison to Model 9, Model 10 explained no more variation in the dependent variable, though. This is not surprising, however, because the only difference between the two models was the introduction of the neighborhood social ties variable, which had already been previously found to explain no additional variance in actual police use of excessive force (Model 8). Furthermore, because the effect of neighborhood social ties was very small in Model 10, and because it was non-significant, it should not be expected to explain any more variation in actual police use of excessive force than in did Model 9.

Despite the lack of support for the systemic model observed in these analyses, the results of Model 10 affirmatively answer the larger research questions presented in Chapter 4 regarding the possibility of a relationship between neighborhood social disorganization and police use of excessive force. That is, with the exception of the systemic model, the evidence presented in this book strongly suggests that the social disorganization tradition is not only a viable theoretical framework for explaining police officers' use of excessive force, but a strong and robust one too. Unfortunately, however, the evidence also confirms the regrettable conclusion that the residents of socially disorganized neighborhoods are indeed more likely to be doubly-victimized with nowhere to turn – first by the criminals who prey on them, and then by police officers who are supposed to protect them.

CHAPTER 7

DISCUSSION & CONCLUSIONS

How and why police officers use force against American civilians has been, and will always continue to be, a controversial topic of much debate. Similarly, it has also been a central focus of past and future of empirical research efforts. The better we understand the intricacies of police use of force behaviors, the more we can do to address the rare, but tremendously consequential, instances of both legitimate and illegitimate police use of force. And, while even the legitimate use of force on civilians can have profound consequences for victims, police officers, and society as a whole, the use of *il*legitimate force by the police can lead to serious racial/ethnic and class-based tensions between communities and the police officers who patrol them. In turn, these tensions may lead to protests, riots, other forms of social violence, and the delegitimazation of police and state authority. With such high stakes, it is no wonder that policing researchers have spent so much time and energy attempting to better understand the situations and people involved (both civilians and officers alike) that give rise to the illegitimate use of force by the police.

The primary goal of this book was to add to our understanding of why police officers use one form of illegitimate force. Specifically, the question of how neighborhood context influences police officers' use of *excessive* force was examined both theoretically and empirically. Consequently, this research has added to our existing understanding of police use of force behaviors by making three primary contributions. First, a detailed review of all the theory-driven empirical research that has been published over the last twenty years shed light on the field's need for further theoretical development and empirical testing. Second, through the utilization of multi-level modeling techniques in ways that had previously been unconsidered, this research also contributed to the continued methodological development of research on police use of force. Finally, and perhaps, most importantly, a new theoretical framework for explaining police use of force behaviors was proposed, empirically analyzed, and observed to be not only a viable explanation, but a strong one as well.

In addition to the overarching goal of contributing to a stronger understanding of police officers' use of force behaviors, there were two other overarching research questions that this book sought to answer. First, it was asked whether or not neighborhood social disorganization might predict police officers' use of excessive force. Second, it was also questioned whether or not neighborhood collective efficacy was the most important social disorganization factor in predicting police officers' use of excessive force. In the remainder of this chapter, the results of the multi-level analyses presented above are discussed in more detail in order to determine exactly how those broader research questions, as well as the more specific hypotheses identified in Chapter 4, should be answered. The theoretical and policy implications of this research are then reviewed. Finally, the limitations of the research presented here are discussed and a number of directions for future research based on those limitations are proposed.

Discussion of Results

In order to answer the two broader research questions reiterated above, a number of multi-level analyses of police officers' use of excessive force were conducted. These analyses tested four sets of hypotheses (see Chapter 4), each incorporating different concepts, or groups of concepts, from the social disorganization tradition. First, it was hypothesized that neighborhood structural disadvantage would be positively related to police officers' use of excessive force (Hypotheses 1a-c). Second, in a test of the systemic model, it was hypothesized that neighborhood social ties would be negatively related to police officers' use of excessive force (Hypothesis 2a). It was further expected that those ties would mediate the relationship between neighborhood structural disadvantage and police use of excessive force (Hypothesis 2b). Third, it was hypothesized that neighborhood collective efficacy would be negatively related to police officers' use of excessive force (Hypothesis 3a). It was expected that neighborhood collective efficacy it would also mediate the neighborhood between structural disadvantage and police use of excessive force (Hypothesis 3b).

Finally, the primary hypothesis stated that, when all the concepts from the social disorganization tradition were included in a single analysis simultaneously, neighborhood collective efficacy would be the strongest predictor of police officers' use of excessive force (Hypothesis 4).

After controlling for a number of individual- and neighborhood-level factors related to civilian perceptions of the police, either full or partial support for three of the four sets of hypotheses was observed (all but Hypotheses 2a-b). Specifically, for the first set of hypotheses, neighborhood structural disadvantage was found to be a very strong predictor of police officers' use of excessive force. The three measures of neighborhood structural disadvantage – neighborhood concentrated disadvantage, concentrated immigration, and residential instability – were all positively and significantly related to the dependent variable. Substantively, these results suggest that neighborhoods with high levels of poverty, racial/ethnic tensions, and turnover should be more likely to experience problems with police use of excessive force, just as the adapted social disorganization theoretical framework proposed in Chapter 4 had predicted. In other words, just as disadvantaged neighborhoods are more vulnerable to crime, they are also more vulnerable to police officers' abuse of authority.

While the relationship between neighborhood structural disadvantage and police officers' use of excessive force was expected, that relationship was also expected to be fully mediated by the effect of neighborhood social ties and collective efficacy – the two mechanisms through which neighborhood structural disadvantage was hypothesized to actually make neighborhoods more vulnerable to both criminals and police officers' use of excessive force. In spite of the theoretical rationale, however, in each of the mediation models that were tested, the effect of neighborhood structural disadvantage remained both strong and significant. Moreover, in the final model, which included neighborhood structural disadvantage, social ties, and collective efficacy simultaneously, the three component measures of neighborhood structural disadvantage were still strong and significant predictors of police officers' use of excessive force. In fact, contrary to expectations, neighborhood concentrated disadvantage actually had a greater influence on police use of excessive force than did neighborhood collective efficacy.

The finding described above suggests that even when holding two popular and commonly tested mediating concepts from the social disorganization tradition constant (neighborhood social ties and collective efficacy), neighborhood structural disadvantage still has a strong, direct effect on police use of excessive force. And, even though this finding challenges several of the hypotheses proposed earlier, it in no ways precludes the viability of a social disorganization theory of police use of force.

On the contrary, the direct relationship between neighborhood structural disadvantage and police officers' use of excessive force suggests only that neighborhood social ties and neighborhood collective efficacy are not the only ecological processes occurring within a neighborhood that might mediate the relationship. For instance, it might be that neighborhoods with high levels of structural disadvantage, which have historically experienced sharp police-community tensions, are more likely to have residents who are more fearful or distrustful of the police. As a result of this fear and distrust, residents may then be unable or unwilling to come together to stand up to the police use of excessive force. Alternatively, residents of structurally disadvantage neighborhoods may be less likely to have the time, knowledge, or other resources (i.e., social capital) necessary to file formal complaints against officers who use excessive force in their neighborhoods.

It may also simply be the case that there is a direct effect of living in a highly disadvantaged neighborhood on police officers' use of excessive force. It is certainly possible that some of the other aspects associated with living in a structurally disadvantaged neighborhood could also signal to police officers that they will be able to get away with the use of excessive force. Using a *broken windows explanation* (Wilson and Kelling 1982), for example, structurally disadvantaged neighborhoods will likely also have high levels of physical (e.g., graffiti, litter, and barred or broken windows) and social (e.g., loitering, panhandling, and public drug use) disorder, which could then also signal both criminals and police officers that their deviant or illegal behavior will not be confronted or controlled.

Unfortunately, an analysis of the physical and social disorder is beyond the scope of this book, but does provide an interesting direction for future research. So, even though the findings obtained in this research challenged the two mediation hypotheses, they nonetheless supported the first set of hypotheses and provide very compelling evidence that neighborhood structural disadvantage is in fact related to police officers' use of excessive force.

In addition to the surprising direct effect of neighborhood structural disadvantage on police use of excessive force, another somewhat unexpected finding of this research was the lack of support for the second set of hypotheses (testing the systemic model). Although some recent research has called into question the importance of neighborhood social ties in determining neighborhood crime rates (Bellair 1997; Browning et al. 2004; Patillo-McCoy 1999; Sampson et al. 1997; Wilson 1996), it was still surprising that the number of close familial and friendship ties that were shared among neighborhood residents had no influence on police officers' use of excessive force. Even in the bivariate tests, neighborhood social ties were found to have no significant impact on police use of excessive force.

Substantively, the findings of this research strongly suggests that social ties within a neighborhood do not affect the likelihood of the neighborhood being able to confront, and put a stop to, police officers' abuse of authority. As a matter of fact, it appears that the number of close friends and family that residents have in their neighborhood is unrelated to police officers' use of excessive force. Instead, the results suggest that it is the sharing of common goals and a mutual trust amongst neighborhood residents that one's neighbors will intervene on behalf of the neighborhood (i.e., collective efficacy) that is the more important factor.

Another surprising result related to the effect of neighborhood social ties was the reversal of the direction of its effect when neighborhood collective efficacy was included in the analyses (see Model 10 in Table 6.4). Even though the effect remained non-significant, and cannot therefore be confidently distinguished from having no effect at all (i.e., a null relationship), it is nonetheless quite interesting that neighborhood social ties went from having a negative relationship with police officers' use of excessive force in all of the previous models to having a positive relationship in the last one. This might mean that, when controlling for neighborhood collective efficacy, the number of close social ties that residents have may actually increase the likelihood that police use of excessive force will become more of a problem.

While the possibility that neighborhoods with strong social networks and high collective efficacy should experience more police use of excessive force may not seem very intuitive, there is one possible explanation. Perhaps when residents have many close social ties in collectively efficacious neighborhoods, a "diffusion of responsibility" (Darley and Latané 1968) effect may occur. That is, individual residents might each expect that the other members of their social networks are going to deal with whatever problems that might arise. Consequently, if each of the residents of a neighborhood relies on his or her neighbors to be the first to step up and handle a problem, then, in the end, it could be that *no one* steps up to handle the problem. In this way, it might then be possible that neighborhoods with many social ties could actually experience an increase in police officers' use of excessive force. Again, however, because the positive relationship between neighborhood social ties and police use of excessive was non-significant in the final model, any real relationship between the two variables cannot be confidently established. Consequently, the results obtained here challenge not only the systemic model hypotheses proposed in this book, but the viability of systemic model explanation of police officers' use of excessive force in general.

In relative comparison to systemic model explanation of police use of excessive force, a collective efficacy explanation appears to be much more feasible based on the analyses testing the third and fourth sets of hypotheses. As discussed in the previous chapter, the results of Models 3, 7, 9 and 10 all suggested that neighborhood collective efficacy is, in fact, a very strong and robust explanation of police officers' use of excessive force behaviors. As was expected, evidence was found not only of a strong negative bivariate relationship (Model 3), but also of a very strong negative relationship when controlling for civilian reporting bias (Model 7), and all of the other concepts from the social disorganization tradition (Models 9 and 10). In fact, across all the models analyzed in this book, neighborhood collective efficacy was consistently one of the strongest (i.e., largest in magnitude) predictors of police officers' use of excessive force.

Despite the strong evidence in support of a collective efficacy explanation of police use of excessive force, however, neighborhood collective efficacy did not completely mediate the relationship between neighborhood structural disadvantage and police officers' use of excessive force, challenging the collective efficacy mediation hypothesis. Moreover, the single measure of neighborhood concentrated disadvantage, as well as the three component measures of neighborhood structural disadvantage as a whole, had larger effects on police officers' use of excessive force, thereby challenging the fourth and final hypothesis, to a degree. Nevertheless, these findings say more about the capacity of neighborhood structural disadvantage to predict police officers' use of excessive force than they do to undermine the importance of neighborhood collective efficacy. That is, because it has one of the strongest relationships with police officers' use of excessive force, net of a host of control and other explanatory variables, the analyses obtained here still provide very compelling evidence that neighborhood collective efficacy can, and should, be considered a very strong and robust predictor of police officers' use of excessive force.

So, what do the findings regarding the relationship between neighborhood collective efficacy and police use of excessive force relationship mean substantively? Simply put, the results of this research do support the argument presented in Chapter 4, even if only partially thus far. Briefly, it was argued that if neighborhood residents shared common goals and values with their neighbors, and if they could count on those neighbors to intervene on behalf of the neighborhood's greater good (i.e., their neighborhood had high level of collective efficacy), then residents would have the power to reduce not only crime, but problems with police officers' use of excessive force as well. It was then further argued that the relationship between neighborhood collective efficacy and police officers' use of excessive force likely operated in a fashion similar to the relationship between neighborhood collective efficacy and crime rates. That is, just as neighborhoods with low collective efficacy signal to potential offenders that they will be able to get away with criminal and deviant behavior, those neighborhoods also signal to police officers that if they use excessive levels of force, there will be no single individual, and especially no larger group (i.e., the entire neighborhood), who will do anything to stop them or get them in trouble. Finally, it was argued that as officers came to realize that the residents of low collective efficacy neighborhoods did not have the ability to stop them, their use of excessive force would increase. And, just as was expected, the results of this research confirmed that levels of neighborhood collective efficacy were indeed negatively related to neighborhood problems with police officers' use of excessive force.[62]

Based on the results obtained in this book, it can therefore be concluded that the social disorganization tradition more generally, and collective efficacy framework in particular, are both viable theoretical explanations for the police use of excessive force. Furthermore, the two broader research questions asked at the beginning of this research can be answered affirmatively. More explicitly, neighborhood social disorganization was indeed related to police officers' use of excessive force, and neighborhood collective efficacy was one of the strongest and most robust predictors among those examined. As such, if one then recalls the well-established relationship between neighborhood social disorganization and rates of crime once again (see Chapter 3), it becomes quite evident that socially disorganized neighborhoods, and especially those with low collective efficacy, are without doubt doubly-victimized – both by the criminals who prey upon them and by the police officers who are supposed to protect them.

---

[62] The theoretical arguments made in this book cannot be entirely substantiated (or falsified, for that matter) because the data utilized in this research did not measure police officers' recognition of neighborhood collective efficacy (or the lack thereof), nor their subsequent thinking in regards to the use of force. Unfortunately, it is beyond the scope of this book to uncover exactly how neighborhood collective efficacy influences police officers' thought processes, and, in fact, there is no existing source of data that could decipher this relationship. Future research should attempt to collect such data and explicate the relationship.

Theoretical and Policy Implications

There are a number of theoretical and policy implications that can be derived from the research presented in this book. First, in regards to the theoretical implications of this research, it should be evident now more than ever that the field of policing needs more theory, and more theory-driven research. This book was intended to help address both such needs, and was generally successful in doing so. That is to say, even though the results of this research focused specifically on the relationship between neighborhood social disorganization and police officers' use of *excessive* force, the fact that a relationship between the two measures was observed should indicate to other policing researchers that other concepts from the social disorganization tradition may be helpful for explaining not only police use of excessive force, but other types of police behavior as well. Furthermore, the fact that a traditionally criminological theory was able to be adapted to propose an entirely new explanation for police officers' use of excessive force should suggest to other policing researchers that more theory is not only needed, but also that it can come from anywhere.

Thus, in addition to demonstrating that the neighborhood social disorganization tradition is a viable theoretical framework for explaining police use of force behavior, it is hoped that this research might also push other policing researchers to propose new theories for explaining police behavior and/or test other existing theories that might be applied to the explanation of police behavior. As reviewed in Chapter 2, there are currently only two empirically supported theoretical frameworks for explaining police officers' use of force – three categories if the results of this research are added to the mix. Taken altogether, however, it is still very unlikely that policing researchers will be able to more fully explain police officers' use of force without expanding their horizons. So, while this research helps further the theoretical development of the field, more theory-driven research is still needed if we are ever to reach a better understanding of why police officers use all types of force – legitimate or otherwise – on civilians and criminals alike.

In terms of the policy implications of this research, several important findings should be considered. First, it may be necessary to more closely monitor the behaviors of police officers working in socially disorganized, and especially low collective efficacy, neighborhoods. As discussed in Chapter 4, although the theoretical arguments underlying this research does not expect that all police officers working in such neighborhoods to abuse their authority and use excessive levels of force more often, it can take the actions of only one rogue officer to create a serious problem for an entire neighborhood. Police administrators should therefore pay careful attention to how their officers behave in disorganized neighborhoods. Through the use of increasingly available advancements in technologies (e.g., patrol car dash cameras, in-car computer systems, and even radio communication systems), an increased focus on officers working in disorganized neighborhoods could allow administrators to monitor potentially dangerous situations and any illegitimate uses of force.

Second, making it easier for neighborhood residents to report problems and ensuring them that the use of excessive force would not only be properly disciplined, but that residents would not need to fear police retaliation could go a long way toward reducing improper behavior in socially disorganized neighborhoods. In other words, by making police officers more accountable for their uses of force, they may think twice before using excessive levels of force. Increasing the ease and safety associated with residents' reporting of police abuses of authority could be achieved in a number of ways. For example, police departments could administer anonymous and confidential surveys to the residents of socially disorganized to assess the extent to which police abuse of force was a problem. Departments might also increase punishments for the improper use of force and make public announcements of those punishments so that neighborhood residents realize that the matter is taken seriously. Or, departments might work with their cities to create external and/or civilian review boards which could be used hold officers accountable.   Whatever the method, increasing police officer accountability and helping civilians easily and safely report problems are two essential elements in reducing police abuse of force problems not only in socially disorganized neighborhoods, but in all types of neighborhoods.

The introduction and development of community-oriented policing and other similar programs into socially disorganized neighborhoods may be a third way to help alleviate problems of police use of excessive force. Community-oriented policing is generally intended to bring police officers and neighborhood residents together to *collectively* define and address neighborhood problems. Such efforts may be even more important in disorganized neighborhoods because residents may not even know their neighbors, let alone the officers who work in their neighborhood. If officers get to know the people they see on a daily basis, they may be less inclined to use excessive force on those people. Moreover, if they can come to understand the people living in disorganized neighborhoods, they may get a better sense of when, and how much, force is necessary to handle a situation. Conversely, the increased use of such programs may actually increase neighborhoods' levels of social *organization* and/or collective efficacy. That is, if neighborhood residents get to know their neighbors and police officers better, they may be more likely to trust each other and work together to fight neighborhood problems (i.e., increase the neighborhood's collective efficacy). Consequently, neighborhoods that were once doubly-victimized may see doubly-beneficial results of having increased levels collective efficacy – decreases in both police use of excessive force *and* decreases in crime rates as well.

Finally, the results of this research should make it even more evident that our society still needs to address the problem of structural disadvantage within inner-cities. Not only is neighborhood structural disadvantage related to crime problems, but as this research shows, it is also directly related to police officers' use of excessive force. Unfortunately, there are no easy solutions for reducing such pervasive and widespread problems related to poverty, racial/ethnic tensions, and residential instability. Many government programs already exist that help individuals improve their job skills, tolerance and acceptance of others, and rates of home ownership. While the results of this research might not help shed any light on more or better methods for addressing these larger problems, it does provide yet another good reason to keep working toward reducing neighborhood structural disadvantage.

Limitations of this Research and Directions for Future Research

While the results of this research provide very compelling evidence that neighborhood social disorganization is strongly and robustly related to police officers' use of excessive force, there are a number of limitations of this research that need to be understood. Unfortunately, the majority of these limitations are related to the specific data used to conduct this research. It should be clear, however, that the PHDCN is not a poor source of data for research on neighborhood context and police use of force behaviors. On the contrary, as discussed in Chapter 5, the PHDCN is an ideal source of data for not only this research, but for many other studies of neighborhoods and policing. The major limitations of the data used in this research are more specifically related to the type of data that were used, rather than anything related distinctly to the PHDCN. Simply put, the major limitations of this research are attributable to the cross-sectional civilian-survey design of the study and its sole focus on Chicago, IL, during the 1990s.

The first, and perhaps most important, limitation of this research is that it relies on civilian respondents' reports of police officers' use of excessive force behaviors. Despite the considerable theoretical and empirical efforts that were taken in order to account for any potential civilian reporting bias in the dependent variable, there will inevitably be some individuals who still consider this research to be pertinent only to civilian perceptions of police behavior, rather than their actual police behaviors.

In an ideal world, data would be available that accurately measures every instance of police officers' uses of excessive force. Unfortunately, in the real world, no such data exist. Furthermore, as reviewed in Chapter 5, there is a small, but significant, body of research that suggests that both police officer self-report and systematic observational data have measurement error issues that can be just as problematic for measuring actual police behavior. Thus, because there is no existing data source that includes entirely accurate measures of police use of force *and* measures of neighborhood context – such as the neighborhood collective efficacy variable that is of primary interest for this research – the PHDCN data is currently the best source of data available. Of course, if data do become available that measures both police use of force using some alternative method (e.g., police officer self-reports or systematic observations) and neighborhood context, future research should attempt to replicate the findings in this research.

A second limitation of this research is the failure to test the newly proposed social disorganization theory of police behavior against the two theoretical frameworks that currently dominate the police use of force literature – the social threat and criminal threat theoretical frameworks. As with the previous limitation, this limitation is also related to the possibility of measurement error issues in the dependent variable used in this research. While a number of the social threat and criminal threat measures that were reviewed in Chapter are available in the PHDCN data, in order to account for any potential civilian reporting bias, it was necessary to use those measures to help reduce the variation in the dependent variable that may have been a result of those factors. For example, the PHDCN data include measures of respondents' race/ethnicity and social class, which could be utilized to test social threat theories. Alternatively, the data also include measures of neighborhood crime rates, which could be utilized to test criminal threat theories. Regrettably, however, based on the nature of the dependent variable in this study, all such measures were utilized to account for the possibility of civilian reporting bias, making it impossible for me to test a social disorganization theory of police use of excessive force against the social threat and criminal threat theoretical frameworks.

Of course, if the effects of race/ethnicity, social class, and neighborhood crime rates on police use of excessive force were to be interpreted using a social threat or criminal threat lens, however, the results of this research would be supportive of both the social threat and criminal threat theoretical frameworks.[63] First, as shown in Table 6.4 in the previous chapter, each of the racial/ethnic minority groups (blacks, Hispanics, Asians, and other race group members) had

---

[63] While the social threat and criminal threat measures that are discussed here were used as controls for civilian reporting bias, for the sake of this hypothetical discussion, their effects are interpreted as if they actually influenced police use of excessive force *behaviors*, rather than influencing respondents' *reports* of police behavior.

significantly greater odds than whites of experiencing problems with police use of excessive force, net of all the other covariates in the model. Table 6.4 also showed that social class was significantly and negatively related to police use of excessive force, net of all the other covariates in the model. Both of these findings support a social threat explanation of police use of excessive force.   Then, in regards to the criminal threat theoretical framework, Table 6.4 also revealed that neighborhood crime rates were significantly and positively related to police officers' use of excessive force, net of all the other covariates in the model. Using an alternative interpretation of the results of this research, a criminal threat explanation could therefore be supported as well.

Thus, if the effects of the variables discussed above were also interpreted as measures of social threat and criminal threat, then this book would be strongly supportive for all three theoretical frameworks (i.e., social threat, criminal threat, and social disorganization). Unfortunately, however, until researchers can disentangle the effects of social threat and criminal threat measures on civilians' *reports of police behaviors* versus *actual police behaviors*, future researchers should attempt to utilize non-civilian-survey data (that does not require them to account for the potential of reporting bias) to test the social disorganization tradition theoretical framework against the two currently dominant theories of police use of force.

A third limitation of this research is its focus on police officers' use of *excessive* force only. While a better understanding of why police officers use excessive levels of force on individuals living in socially disorganized neighborhoods is extremely valuable, it would be advantageous if researchers knew whether or not neighborhood social disorganization influenced other types of police use of force as well. Earlier in this research, it was argued that socially disorganized and low collective efficacy neighborhoods might experience more police use of excessive force because they lacked the collective capacity to put a stop to deviant behavior, whether it was crime or the abuse of police authority. However, it could also be argued that socially organized and high collective efficacy neighborhoods could reduce the amount of *legitimately* used police force as well. That is, such organized and collectively effective neighborhoods might not only be able to prevent police abuse of force, but they might also have the social, political, and/or financial capital to influence how police officers use even the most justified forms of forceful behaviors. Future research should test this informal hypothesis to help further our understanding of how and why neighborhood context influences police officers' use of force.

A fourth limitation of this research relates to the cross-sectional design of the PHDCN data. Because the relationship between neighborhood social disorganization and police officers' use of excessive force was examined using data from the same timeframe, it is not possible to truly determine the temporal sequencing of events. In other words, true causality cannot be accurately established. Is it really neighborhood social disorganization that influences police officers' use of excessive force? Or, is it possible that police use of excessive force contributes to neighborhoods becoming socially disorganized? While the latter scenario might be unlikely, it is conceivable that neighborhood problems with the police use of excessive force might cause residents to stay in their homes to avoid the police, which, in turn, might lead to residents being unable to get to know each other and form common goals, ultimately leading to more neighborhood social disorganization and less neighborhood collective efficacy. Thus, in order to determine whether or not neighborhood social disorganization truly causes police officers to use excessive levels of force, longitudinal data with measures of disorganization at one time and police use of excessive force at a later time are necessary. Unfortunately, no such data yet exists, but its collection would be a very promising avenue for future research.

And so, even if the temporal nature of the relationship between social disorganization tradition and police use of force behavior cannot be empirically assessed in this research, it is still quite valuable in terms of establishing that a relationship between the two phenomena actually exists. Then, if one accepts the theoretical arguments for why neighborhood social disorganization should influence police officers' use of force that were laid out in Chapter 4, there is also sound justification for the general conclusion that neighborhood social disorganization does in fact predict police officers' use of excessive force. Future research should nonetheless attempt to verify the arguments and mechanisms proposed in this book using longitudinal data as well.

One final limitation of this research regards the generalizability of its findings to other times and locations. Because the PHDCN data is limited to Chicago neighborhoods during the mid-1990s, it is not clear whether the findings presented here can be generalized to other cities or other time periods. Although the city of Chicago served as the inspiration and source of data for nearly every significant contribution to the social disorganization tradition, and is therefore appropriate for any tests of the tradition, the unique history and nature of the city (i.e., its numerous riots that resulted from police officers' use of force and the extensive socioeconomic and racial/ethnic diversity) make it different from most of the other cities throughout the country. Thus, future research should examine relationships between neighborhood context and police use of force in a variety of locales and at a variety of different time periods in order to determine whether the findings of this research are specific only to Chicago in the mid-1990s, or if socially disorganized neighborhoods across both space and time have been, are currently being, or will be in the future, doubly-victimized by high levels of crime and police use of excessive force with nowhere else to turn.

All things considered, however, the theory, methods, and findings presented in this book provide compelling evidence that neighborhood social disorganization is indeed related to police officers' use of force. If future research can address some the limitations discussed here, perhaps even more firm conclusions can be drawn. In the meantime, however, if there is even a possibility that residents of socially disorganized neighborhoods really do have nowhere to turn because they are being doubly-victimized by both criminals and the police officers who are supposed to protect them, as this book suggests they are, then a new option to which those residents can turn needs to be found.

APPENDIX

Project on Human Development in Chicago Neighborhoods: Community Survey, 1994-1995, Selected Instrument Items

Neighborhood Collective Efficacy Measures

Social Cohesion Measures

"For each of these statements, please tell me whether you strongly agree, agree, disagree, or strongly disagree."

Q11A   This is a close-knit neighborhood.
Q11E   People around here are willing to help their neighbors.
Q11F   People in this neighborhood don't generally get along with each other (reverse-coded).
Q11J   In this neighborhood people mostly go their own way (reverse-coded).
Q11K   People in this neighborhood do not share the same values (reverse-coded).
Q11M   People in this neighborhood can be trusted.

Informal Social Control Measures

"For each of the following, please tell me if it is very likely, likely, unlikely, or very unlikely that people in your neighborhood would act in the following manner."

Q12A   If a group of neighborhood children were skipping school and hanging out on a street corner, how likely is it that your neighbors would do something about it?
Q12B   If some children were spray-painting graffiti on a local building, how likely is it that your neighbors would do something about it?

Q12C   If a child was showing disrespect to an adult,
         how likely is it that people in your neighborhood
         would scold that child?
Q12E   If there was a fight in front of your house and
         someone was being beaten or threatened, how
         likely is it that your neighbors would break it up?

Neighborhood Social Ties Measures (Systemic Model)

"Not counting those who live with you . . . "

Q17a   How many of your relatives or in-laws live in
         your neighborhood? Would you say none, one
         or two, three to five, six to nine, or ten or more?
Q17b   How many of your friends do you have in your
         neighborhood? Would you say none, one or two,
         three to five, six to nine, or ten or more?

Legal Cynicism Measures

"I am going to read you some statements people sometimes make.
For each, please tell me whether you strongly agree, agree,
disagree, or strongly disagree with each."

Q41A   Laws were made to be broken.
Q41B   It's okay to do anything you want as long as you
         don't hurt anyone
Q41C   To make money, there are no right and wrong
         ways anymore, only easy ways and hard ways
Q41D   Fighting between friends or within families is
         nobody else's business
Q41F   Nowadays a person has to live pretty much for
         today and let tomorrow take care of itself.

Past Victimization Measures

"While you have lived in this neighborhood . . . "

Q31   Has anyone ever used *violence, such as in a*
            mugging, fight, or sexual assault against you or any
            member of your household anywhere in your
            neighborhood?
Q32   Has your *home ever been broken into*?
Q33   Have you or another member of your household had
            anything stolen from your yard, porch, garage, or
            elsewhere outside your home (but on your
            property)?
Q34   Have you or another member of your household had
            property damaged, including damage to vehicles
            parked in the street, to the outside of your home, or
            to other personal property?

REFERENCES

Adams, Kenneth. 1996. "Measuring the Prevalence of Police Abuse of Force." In W.A. Geller & H. Toch (eds.) *Police Violence: Understanding and Controlling Police Abuse of Force*, pp. 52-93. New Haven, CT: Yale University Press.

Alpert, Geoffrey P. and John M. MacDonald. 2001. "Police Use of Force: An Analysis of Organizational Characteristics." *Justice Quarterly* 18:393-409.

Anderson, Elijah. 1999. *Code of the Street: Decency, Violence, and the Moral Life of the Inner City.* New York, NY: W.W. Norton.

Bellair, Paul E. 1997. "Social Interaction and Community Crime: Examining the Importance of Neighborhood Networks." *Criminology* 25:677-703.

Bernard, Thomas J. and Robin Shepard Engel. 2001. "Conceptualizing Criminal Justice Theory." *Justice Quarterly* 18:1-30.

Biderman, Albert D. and James P. Lynch. 1991. *Understanding Crime Incidence Statistics: Why the UCR Diverges from the NCS.* New York: Springer-Verlag.

Binder, Arnold and Lorie A. Fridell. 1984. "Lethal Force as a Police Response." *Criminal Justice Abstracts* 16: 250-280

Binder, Arnold and Peter Scharf. 1982. "Deadly Force in Law Enforcement." *Crime and Delinquency* 28:1-23.

Black, Donald. 1976. *The Behavior of Law.* Orlando, FL: Academic Press.

Blalock, Hubert. 1967. *Toward a Theory of Minority-Group Relations.* New York, NY: Capricorn Books.

Blumberg, Mark. 1986. "Issues and Controversies with Respect to the Use of Deadly Force by the Police." In T. Barker and D.L. Carter (eds.) *Police Deviance*, pp. 222-244. Cincinnati, OH: Pilgrimage Press.

Blumer, Herbert. 1958. "Race Prejudice as a Sense of Group Position." *Pacific Sociological Review* 23:3-7.

Bobo, Lawrence and Vincent Hutchings. 1996. "Perceptions of Racial Group Competition: Extending Blumer's Theory of Group Position to a Multiracial Social Context." *American Sociological Review* 61:951-972.

Bordua, David J. and Larry L. Tifft. 1971. "Citizen Interviews, Organizational Feed-Back, and Police-Community Relations Decisions." *Law and Society Review* 6:155-182.

Brown, Ben and Wm Reed Benedict. 2002. "Perceptions of the Police." *Policing* 25:543-82.

Browning, Christopher R. 2002. "The Span of Collective Efficacy: Extending Social Disorganization Theory to Partner Violence." *Journal of Marriage and Family* 64:833-850.

Browning, Christopher R., Seth L. Feinberg, Robert D. Dietz. 2004. "The Paradox of Social Organization: Networks, Collective Efficacy, and Violent Crime in Urban Neighborhoods." *Social Forces* 83:503-534.

Bursik, Robert J., Jr. 1999. "The Informal Control of Crime through Neighborhood Networks." *Sociological Focus* 32:85-97.

Bursik, Robert J., Jr. and Harold G. Grasmick. 1993. *Neighborhoods and Crime: The Dimensions of Effective Community Control.* New York, NY: Lexington Books.

Cancino, Jeffrey Michael. 2005. "The Utility of Social Capital and Collective Efficacy: Social Control Policy in Nonmetropolitan Settings." *Criminal Justice Policy Review* 16:287-318.

Cao, Liqun, James Frank, and Francis T. Cullen. 1996. "Race, Community Context and Confidence in the Police." *American Journal of Police* 15:3-22.

Carter, David L. 1985. "Hispanic Perception of Police Performance: An Empirical Assessment." *Journal of Criminal Justice* 13:487-500.

Chamlin, Mitchell B. 1989. "Conflict Theory and Police Killings." *Deviant Behavior* 10:353-368.

Chappell, Allison T. and Alex R. Piquero. 2004. "Applying Social Learning Theory to Police Misconduct." *Deviant Behavior* 25:89-108.

Copeland, Arthur R. 1986. "Police Shootings: The Metropolitan Dad County Experience from 1956 to 1982." *American Journal of Forensic Medicine and Pathology* 7:39-45.

Correia, Mark E., Michael D. Reisig, and Nicholas P. Lovrich. 1996. "Public Perceptions of State Police: An Analysis of Individual-Level and Contextual Variables." *Journal of Criminal Justice* 24:17-28.

Correll, Joshua, Bernadette Park, Charles M. Judd, and Bernd Wittenbrink. 2002. "The Police Officer's Dilemma: Using Ethnicity to Disambiguate Potentially Threatening Individuals." *Journal of Personality and Social Psychology* 83:1314-1329.

Correll, Joshua, Bernadette Park, Charles M. Judd, Bernd Wittenbrink, Melody S. Sadler, Tracie Keesee. 2007. "Across the Thin Blue Line: Police Officers and Racial Bias in the Decision to Shoot." *Journal of Personality and Social Psychology* 92:1006-1023.

Correll, Joshua, Geoffrey R. Urland, and Tiffany A. Ito. 2006. "Event-Related Potentials and the Decision to Shoot: The Role of Threat Perception and Cognitive Control." *Journal of Experimental Social Psychology* 42:120-128.

Culliver, Concetta and Robert Sigler. 1995. "Police Use of Deadly Force in Tennessee Following Tennessee v. Garner." *Journal of Contemporary Criminal Justice* 11:187-195.

Darley, John M. and Bibb Latané. 1968. "Bystander Intervention in Emergencies: Diffusion of Responsibility." *Journal of Personality and Social Psychology* 58:377-383.

Davis, John R. 1990. "A Comparison of Attitudes toward the New York City Police." *Journal of Police Science and Administration* 17:233-243.

Dean, Debby. 1980. "Citizen Ratings of the Police: The Difference Contact Makes." *Law and Police Quarterly* 2:445-471.

Decker, Scott H. 1981. "Citizen Attitudes toward the Police: A Review of Past Findings and Suggestions for Future Policy." *Journal of Police Science and Administration* 9:80-87.

Dwyer, William O., Arthur C. Graesser, Patricia L. Hopkinson, and Michael B. Lupfer. 1990. "Application of Script Theory to Police Officers' Use of Deadly Force." *Journal of Police Science and Administration* 17:295-301.

Earls, Felton J., Jeanne Brooks-Gunn, Stephen W. Raudenbush, and Robert J. Sampson. 1997. *Project on Human Development in Chicago Neighborhoods: Community Survey, 1994-1995.* Boston, MA: Harvard Medical School.

Elicker, Matthew K. 2008. "Unlawful Justice: An Opinion Study on the Police Use of Force and How Views Change Based on Race and Occupation." *Sociological Viewpoints* 24:33-50.

Fyfe, James J. 1988. "Police Use of Deadly Force: Research and Reform." *Justice Quarterly* 5:165-205.

------. 1980. "Geographic Correlates of Police Shooting: A Microanalysis." *Journal of Research in Crime and Delinquency* 17:101-113.

------. 1979. "Administrative Interventions on Police Shooting Discretion: An Empirical Examination." *Journal of Criminal Justice* 7:309-323.

Garner, Joel H., Christopher D. Maxwell, and Cedrick G. Heraux. 2002. "Characteristics Associated with the Prevalence and Severity of Force Used by the Police." *Justice Quarterly* 19:705-746.

Garner, Joel H., Thomas Schade, John Hepburn, and John Buchanan. 1995. "Measuring the Continuum of Force Used By and Against the Police." *Criminal Justice Review* 20:146-169.

Geller, William A. and Hans Toch. 1996. *Police Violence: Understanding and Controlling Police Abuse of Force.* New Haven, CT: Yale University Press.

Goldkamp, John S. 1976. "Minorities as Victims of Police Shootings: Interpretations of Racial Disproportionality and Police Use of Deadly Force." *Justice System Journal* 2:169-183.

Gove, Walter, Michael Hughes, and Michael Geerken. 1985. "Are Uniform Crime Reports a Valid Indicator the Index Crimes? An Affirmative Answer with Minor Qualifications." *Criminology* 23:451-502.

Granovetter, Mark S. 1973. "The Strength of Weakness Ties." *American Journal of Sociology* 78:1360-1380.

Greenwald, Anthony G., Mark A. Oakes, and Hunter G. Hoffman. 2003. "Targets of Discrimination: Effects of Race on Responses to Weapons Holders." *Journal of Experimental Social Psychology* 39:399-405.

Hadar, Ilana and John R. Snortum. 1975. "The Eye of the Beholder: Differential Perceptions of Police by the Police and by the Public." *Criminal Justice and Behavior* 2:37-54.

Hagan, John. 1989. "Why is There So Little Criminal Justice Theory? Neglected Macro- and Micro-Level Links between Organization and Power." *Journal of Research in Crime and Delinquency* 25:116-135.

Hagan, John and Celesta Albonetti. 1982. "Race, Class, and the Perception of Criminal Justice in America." *American Journal of Sociology* 88:329-355.

Halim, Shaheen, and Beverly L. Stiles. 2001. "Differential Support for Police Use of Force, the Death Penalty, and Perceived Harshness of the Courts: Effects of Race, Gender, and Region." *Criminal Justice and Behavior* 28:3-23.

Hayden, George A. 1981. "Police Discretion in the Use of Deadly Force: An Empirical Study of Information Usage in Deadly Force Decision Making." *Journal of Police Science and Administration* 9:102-107.

Helsen, Werner F. and Janet L. Starkes. 1999. "A New Training Approach to Complex Decision Making for Police Officers in Potentially Dangerous Interventions: Police Use of Deadly Force." *Journal of Criminal Justice* 24:395-410.

Holmes, Malcolm D. 2000. "Minority Threat and Police Brutality: Determinants of Civil Rights Complaints in U.S. Municipalities." *Criminology* 38:343-368.

Holmes, Stephen T., Michael K. Reynolds, Ronald M. Holmes, and Samuel Faulkner. 1998. "Individual and Situational Determinants of Police Force: An Examination of Threat Presentation." *American Journal of Criminal Justice* 23:83-106.

Homant, Robert J., Daniel B. Kennedy, and Roger M. Fleming. 1984. "The Effect of Victimization and the Police Response on Citizens' Attitudes toward Police." *Journal of Police Science & Administration* 12:323-332.

Horvath, Frank. 1987. "The Police Use of Deadly Force: A Description of Selected Characteristics of Intrastate Incidents." *Journal of Police Science and Administration* 15:226-238.

Hunter, Albert J. 1985. "Private, Parochial and Public School Orders: The Problem of Crime and Incivility in Urban Communities." In G.D. Suttles and M.N. Zald (eds.), *The Challenge of Social Control: Citizenship and Institution Building in Modem Society*, pp. 230-242. Norwood, N.J.: Ablex Publishing.

Jacob, Herbert. 1971. "Black and White Perceptions of Justice in the City." *Law and Society Review* 6:69-89.

Jacobs, David. 1979. "Inequality and Police Strength: Conflict Theory and Coercive Control in Metropolitan Areas." *American Sociological Review* 44:913-925.

Jacobs, David and David Britt. 1979. "Inequality and Police Use of Deadly Force: An Empirical Assessment of a Conflict Hypothesis." *Social Problems* 26:403-412.

Jacobs, David and Robert M. O'Brien. 1998. "The Determinants of Deadly Force: A Structural Analysis of Police Violence." *American Journal of Sociology* 103:837-862.

Jefferis, Eric S., Robert J. Kaminski, Stephen Holmes, and Dena E. Hanley. 1997. "The Effect of a Videotaped Arrest on Public Perceptions of Police Use." *Journal of Criminal Justice* 25:381-395.

Johnson, Devon and Joseph B. Kuhns. 2009. "Striking Out: Race and Support for Police Use of Force." *Justice Quarterly* 26:592-623.

Kaminski, Robert J. and Eric S. Jefferis. 1998. "The Effect of a Violent Televised Arrest on Public Perceptions of the Police: A Partial Test of Easton's Theoretical Framework." *Policing: An International Journal of Police Strategies & Management* 21:683-706.

Kane, Robert J. 2002. "The Social Ecology of Police Misconduct."
Criminology 40:867-896.

Kania, Richard E. and Wade C. Mackey. 1977. "Police Violence as a Function
of Community Characteristics." *Criminology* 15:27-48.

Kasarda, John D. and Morris Janowitz. 1974. "Community Attachment in
Mass Society." *American Sociological Review* 39:328-339.

Klinger, David A. 2004. "Environment and Organization: Reviving a
Perspective on the Police." *Annals of the American Academy of Political
and Social Science* 593:119-136.

------. 1997. "Negotiating Order in Patrol Work: An Ecological Theory of
Police Response to Deviance." *Criminology* 35:277–306.

Kornhauser, Ruth Rosner. 1978. *Social Sources of Delinquency: An Appraisal
of Analytic Models.* Chicago, IL: University of Chicago Press.

Krivo, Lauren J. and Ruth D. Peterson. 1996. "Extremely Disadvantaged
Neighborhoods and Urban Crime." *Social Forces* 75: 619-650.

Lawton, Brian A. 2007. "Levels of Nonlethal Force: An Examination of
Individual, Situational, and Contextual Factors." *Journal of Research in
Crime and Delinquency* 44:163-184.

Lee, Barrett A. and Karen E. Campbell. 1997. "Common Ground? Urban
Neighborhoods as Survey Respondents See Them." *Social Science
Quarterly* 78:922-936.

Lersch, Kim M., Thomas Bazley, Thomas Mieczkowski, and Kristina Childs.
2008. "Police Use of Force and Neighbourhood Characteristics: An
Examination of Structural Disadvantage, Crime, and Resistance."
Policing & Society 18:282-300.

Liska, Allen E. and Jiang Yu. 1992. "Specifying and Testing the Threat
Hypothesis: Police Use of Deadly Force." In A.E. Liska (ed.), *Social
Threat and Social Control,* pp. 53-68. Albany, NY: State University of
New York Press.

Lowencamp, Christopher T., Francis T. Cullen, and Travis C. Pratt. 2003.
"Replicating Sampson and Groves's Test of Social Disorganization
Theory: Revisiting a Criminological Classic." *Journal of Research in
Crime and Delinquency* 40:351-373.

MacDonald, John M., Geoffrey P. Alpert, and Abraham N. Tennenbaum.
1999. "Justifiable Homicide by Police and Criminal Homicide: A
Research Note." *Journal of Crime and Justice* 22:153-166.

MacDonald, John M., Robert J. Kaminski, Geoffrey P. Alpert, and Abraham N. Tennenbaum. 2001. "The Temporal Relationship between Police Killings of Civilians and Criminal Homicide: A Redefined Version of the Danger-Perception Theory." *Crime & Delinquency* 47:155-172.

MacDonald, John M., Patrick W. Manz, Geoffrey P. Alpert, and Roger G. Dunham. 2003. "Police Use of Force: Examining the Relationship between Calls for Service and the Balance of Police Force and Suspect Resistance." *Journal of Criminal Justice* 31:119-127.

Marenin, Otwin. 1989. "The Utility of Community Needs Surveys in Community Policing." *Police Studies* 12:73-81.

Mastrofski, Stephen and Roger B. Parks. 1990. "Improving Observational Studies of Police." *Criminology* 28:475-496.

McLaughlin, Lindsay M., Shane D. Johnson, Kate J. Bowers, Dan J. Birks, and Ken Pease. 2007. "Police Perceptions of the Long- and Short-Term Spatial Distribution of Residential Burglary." *International Journal of Police Science and Management* 9:99-111.

Meyer, Marshall W. 1980. "Police Shootings at Minorities: The Case of Los Angeles." *Annals of the American Academy of Political and Social Science* 452:98-110.

Micucci, Anthony J. and Ian M. Gomme. 2005. "American Police and Subcultural Support for the Use of Excessive Force." *Journal of Criminal Justice* 33:487-500.

Morenoff, Jeffrey D., Robert J. Sampson, and Stephen W. Raudenbush. 2001. "Neighborhood Inequality, Collective Efficacy, and the Spatial Dynamics of Urban Violence." *Criminology* 39:517-559.

Murty, Komanduri S., Julian B. Roebuck, and Joann E. Smith. 1990. "The Image of the Police in Black Atlanta Communities." *Journal of Police Science and Administration* 17:250-257.

O'Brien, Robert M. 1985. *Crime and Victimization Data.* Beverly Hills, CA: Sage.

Park, Robert E., Ernest W. Burgess, and Roderick D. McKenzie. 1925. *The City.* Chicago, IL: University of Chicago Press.

Parks, Roger B. 1984. "Linking Objective and Subjective Measures of Performance." *Public Administration Review* 44:118-27.

------. 1982. "Citizen Surveys for Police Performance Assessments: Some Issues in Their Use." *The Urban Interest* 4:17-26.

Patillo-McCoy, Mary. 1999. *Black Picket Fences: Privilege and Peril Among the Black Middle Class.* Chicago, IL: University of Chicago Press.

Percy, Stephen L. 1986. "In Defense of Citizen Evaluations as Performance Measures." *Urban Affairs Quarterly* 22:66-83.

------. 1980. "Response Time and Citizen Evaluation of Police." *Journal of Police Science and Administration* 8:75-86.

Peterson, Ruth D., Lauren J. Krivo, and Mark A. Harris. 2000. "Disadvantage and Neighborhood Violent Crime: Do Local Institutions Matter?" *Journal of Research in Crime and Delinquency* 37:31-63.

Raudenbush, Stephen W. and Anthony S. Bryk. 2002. *Hierarchical Linear Models: Applications and Data Analysis Methods, Second Edition.* Thousand Oaks, CA: Sage.

Raudenbush, Stephen W. and Robert J. Sampson. 1999. "Ecometrics: Toward a Science of Assessing Ecological Settings, with Applications to the Systemic Social Observation of Neighborhoods." *Sociological Methodology* 29:1-41.

Reisig, Michael D. and Roger B. Parks. 2000. "Experience, Quality of Life, and Neighborhood Context: A Hierarchical Analysis of Satisfaction with Police." *Justice Quarterly* 17:607-630.

Reisig, Michael D. and Jeffrey Michael Cancino. 2004. "Incivilities in Nonmetropolitan Communities: The Effects of Structural Constraints, Social Conditions, and Crime." *Journal of Criminal Justice* 32:15-29.

Reisig, Michael D. and Andrew L. Giacomazzi. 1998. "Citizen Perceptions of Community Policing: Are Attitudes Toward Police Important." *Policing: An International Journal of Police Strategies & Management* 20:311-325.

Rengart, George F. 1995. "Comparing Cognitive Hotspots to Crime Hotspots." In C. Block, M. Daboub, and S. Fregly (eds.), *Crime Analysis through Computer Mapping*, pp. 33-47. Chicago, IL: Police Executive Research Forum.

Sampson, Robert J. and W. Byron Groves. 1989. "Community Structure and Crime: Testing Social Disorganization Theory. *American Journal of Sociology* 94:774-802.

Sampson, Robert J. and Dawn Jeglum-Bartusch. 1998. "Legal Cynicism and Subcultural? Tolerance of Deviance: The Neighborhood Context of Racial Differences." *Law & Society Review* 32:777–804.

Sampson, Robert J., Jeffrey D. Morenoff, and Felton Earls. 1999. "Beyond Social Capital: Spatial Dynamics of Collective Efficacy for Children." *American Sociological Review* 64:633-660.

Sampson, Robert J., Jeffrey D. Morenoff, and Thomas Gannon-Rowley. 2002. "Assessing 'Neighborhood Effects': Social Processes and New Directions in Research." *Annual Review of Sociology* 28:443-478.

Sampson, Robert J., Stephen W. Raudenbush, and Felton Earls. 1997. "Neighborhoods and Violent Crime: A Multilevel Study of Collective Efficacy." *Science* 277:918-924.

Schafer, Joseph A., Beth M. Huebner, and Timothy S. Bynum. 2003. "Citizen Perceptions of Police Services: Race, Neighborhood Context, and Community Policing." *Police Quarterly* 6:440-468.

Shaw, Clifford R. Henry D. McKay. 1942. *Juvenile Delinquency in Urban Areas.* Chicago, IL: University of Chicago Press.

Sherman, Lawrence W. 1986. "Policing Communities: What Works?" in A.J. Reiss, Jr. and M. Tonry (eds.), *Communities and Crime,* pp. 343-386. Chicago, IL: University of Chicago Press.

Sherman, Lawrence W., Patrick R. Gartin, and Michael E. Buerger. 1989. "Hot Spots of Predatory Crime: Routine Activities and the Criminology of Place." *Criminology* 27:27-56.

Sherman, Lawrence W. and Robert H. Langworthy. 1979. "Measuring Homicide by Police Officers." *Journal of Criminal Law and Criminology* 70:546-560.

Sherman, Lawrence W. and Mark Blumberg. 1981. "Higher Education and Police Use of Deadly Force." *Journal of Criminal Justice* 9:317-331.

Silver, Eric. 2000. "Extending Social Disorganization Theory: A Multi-Level Approach to the Study of Violence Among Discharged Psychiatric Patients." *Criminology* 38:1043-1074.

Silver, Eric and Lisa L. Miller. 2004. "Sources of Informal Social Control in Chicago Neighborhoods." *Criminology* 42:551-583.

Skolnick, Jerome. 1966. *Justice without Trial: Law Enforcement in Democratic Society.* New York, NY: Wiley.

Slovak, Jeffrey. 1986. *Styles of Urban Policing.* New York: New York University Press.

Smith, Douglas A. 1986. "The Neighborhood Context of Police Behavior." In A.J. Reiss, Jr. and M. Tonry (eds.), *Communities and Crime*, pp. 313–41 Chicago: University of Chicago Press.

Smith, Paul E. and Richard O. Hawkins. 1973. "Victimization, Types of Citizen-Police Contacts, and Attitudes Toward the Police." *Law and Society Review* 8:135-152.

Smith, Brad W. and Malcolm D. Holmes. 2003. "Community Accountability, Minority Threat, and Police Brutality: An Examination of Civil Rights Criminal Complaints." *Criminology* 41:1035-1063.

Son, In Soo and Dennis M. Rome. 2004. "The Prevalence and Visibility of Misconduct: A Survey of Citizens and Police Officers." *Police Quarterly* 7:179-204.

Sorensen, Jonathan R., James W. Marquart, and Deon E. Brock. 1993. "Factors Related to Killings of Felons by Police Officers: A Test of the Community Violence and Conflict Hypotheses." *Justice Quarterly* 10:417-440.

South, Scott J. and Kyle D. Crowder. 1997. "Escaping Distressed Neighborhoods: Individual, Community, and Metropolitan Influences." *American Journal of Sociology* 102:1040-1084.

Spano, Richard. 2006. "Observer Behavior as a Potential Source of Reactivity: Describing and Quantifying Observer Effects in a Large-Scale Observational Study of Police." *Sociological Methods & Research* 34:521-553.

------. 2005. "Potential Sources of Observer Bias in Police Observational Data." *Social Science Research* 34:591-617.

Spano, Richard and Michael D. Reisig. 2006. "'Drop the Clipboard and Help Me!': The Determinants of Observer Behavior in Police Encounters with Suspects." *Journal of Criminal Justice* 34:619-629.

Sparger, Jerry R. and David J. Giacopassi. 1992. "Memphis Revisited: A Reexamination of Police Shooting After the Garner Decision." *Justice Quarterly* 9:211-225.

Sun, Ivan Y., Ruth Triplett, and Randy R. Gainey. 2004. "Neighborhood Characteristics and Crime: A Test of Sampson and Groves' Model of Social Disorganization." *Western Criminology Review* 5:1-16.

Tennenbaum, Abraham N. 1994. "The Influence of the Garner Decision on Police Use of Deadly Force." *Journal of Criminal Law and Criminology* 81:241-260.

Terrill, William and Stephen D. Mastrofski. 2002. "Situational and Officer Based Determinants of Police Coercion." *Justice Quarterly* 19:101–34.

Terrill, William, Eugene A. Paoline, III, and Peter K. Manning. 2003. "Police Culture and Coercion." *Criminology* 41:1003-1034.

Terrill, William and Michael D. Reisig. 2003. "Neighborhood Context and Police Use of Force." *Journal of Research in Crime and Delinquency* 40:291-321.

Thompson, Brian L. and James Daniel Lee. 2004. "Who Cares if Police Become Violent? Explaining Approval of Police Use of Force Using a National Sample." *Sociological Inquiry* 74:381-410.

Thurman, Quint C. and Michael D. Reisig. 1996. "Community-Oriented Research in an Era of Community Policing." *American Behavioral Scientist* 39:570-586.

Tienda, Marta. 1991. "Poor People and Poor Places Deciphering Neighborhood Effects on Poverty Outcomes." In J. Huber (ed.), Macro-*Micro Linkages in Sociology.* Newbury Park, CA: Sage.

Triplett, Ruth A., Randy R. Gainey, and Ivan Y. Sun. 2003. "Institutional Strength, Social Control and Neighborhood Crime Rates." *Theoretical Criminology* 7:439-467.

Tuch, Stephen A. and Ronald Weitzer. 1997. "The Polls: Racial Differences in Attitudes Toward the Police." *Public Opinion Quarterly* 61:642-664.

United States Census Bureau. 2008. "An Older and More Diverse Nation by Midcentury." Retrieved September 17, 2009, from http://www.census.gov/newsroom/releases/archives/population/cb08-123.html.

United States Department of Justice. 2005. *Contacts between Police and the Public: Findings from the 2002 National Survey.* Bureau of Justice Statistics.

Velez, Maria B. 2001. "The Role of Public Social Control in Urban Neighborhoods: A Multi-level Analysis of Victimization Risks." *Criminology* 36:441-479.

Veysey, Bonita M. and Steven F. Messner. 1999. "Further Testing of Social Disorganization Theory: An Elaboration of Sampson and Groves's 'Community Structure and Crime'." *Journal of Research in Crime and Delinquency* 36:156-174.

Waegel, William B. 1984a. "The Use of Lethal Force by Police: The Effect of Statutory Change." *Crime and Delinquency* 30:121-140.

------. 1984b. "How Police Justify the Use of Deadly Force." *Social Problems* 32:144-155.

Walker, Samuel and Lorie Fridell. 1992. "Forces of Change in Police Policy: The Impact of Tennessee v. Garner." *American Journal of Police* 11:97-112.

Warner, Barbara D. 2003. "The Role of Attenuated Culture in Social Disorganization Theory." *Criminology* 41:73-98.

Warner, Barbara D. and Glenn L. Pierce. 1993. "Reexamining Social Disorganization Theory Using Calls to the Police as a Measure of Crime." *Criminology* 31:493-517.

Warner, Barbara D. and Pamela Wilcox Rountree. 1997. "Local Social Ties in a Community and Crime Model: Questioning the Systemic Nature of Informal Social Control." *Social Problems* 44:520-536.

Webb, Vincent J. and Chris E. Marshall. 1995. "The Relative Importance of Race and Ethnicity on Citizen Attitudes Toward the Police." *American Journal of Police* 14:45-66.

Weitzer, Ronald. 2002. "Incidents of Police Misconduct and Public Opinion." *Journal of Criminal Justice* 30:397-408.

------. 2000. "White, Black, or Blue Cops? Race and Citizen Assessments of Police Officers." *Journal of Criminal Justice* 28:313-324.

------. 1999. "Citizens' Perceptions of Police Misconduct: Race and Neighborhood Context." *Justice Quarterly* 16:819-46.

Weitzer, Ronald and Steven A. Tuch. 2005. "Determinants of Public Satisfaction with the Police." *Police Quarterly* 8:279-297.

------. 2004. "Race and Perceptions of Police Misconduct." *Social Problems* 51:305-325.

Wilson, James Q. and George L. Kelling. 1982. "Broken Windows: The Police and Neighborhood Safety." *The Atlantic Monthly* 249:29-38.

Wilson, William Julius. 1996. *When Work Disappears: The World of the New Urban Poor.* New York, NY: Vintage Books.

Worden, Robert E. 1996. "The Causes of Police Brutality: Theory and Evidence on Police Use of Force." In W.A. Geller and H. Toch (eds.), *Police Violence: Understanding and Controlling Police Abuse of Force,* pp. 23-51. New Haven, CT: Yale University Press.

Worrall, John L. 1999. "Public Perceptions of Police Efficacy and Image: The 'Fuzziness' of Support for the Police." *American Journal of Criminal Justice* 24:47-66.

INDEX